Inflation, Unemployment and Money

Inflation, Unemployment and Money

Interpretations of the Phillips Curve

Bruno Jossa

Professor of Political Economy
University of Naples, Italy

Marco Musella

Assistant Professor of Political Economy
University of Naples, Italy

Edward Elgar

Cheltenham, UK • Northampton, MA, USA

Published by
Edward Elgar Publishing Limited
Glensanda House
Montpellier Parade
Cheltenham
Glos GL50 1UA
UK

Edward Elgar Publishing, Inc.
6 Market Street
Northampton
Massachusetts 01060
USA

Translation by Aloisia Rigotti

A catalogue record for this book
is available from the British Library

Library of Congress Cataloguing in Publication Data

Jossa, Bruno.
     Inflation, unemployment and money: interpretations
of the Phillips curve / Bruno Jossa, Marco Musella.
     Includes bibliographical references and index.
     1. Phillips curve. 2. Unemployment—Effect of
inflation on—Mathematical models. 3. Neoclassical
school of economics. 4. Keynesian economics.
     I. Musella, Marco, 1960–   . II. Title.
HD5710.2.J67   1998
331.13'7—dc21   98–34327
                                                                              CIP

ISBN 1 85898 457 2

Printed and bound in Great Britain by Bookcraft (Bath) Ltd.

Contents

List of Figures and Tables

Tables

Preface

The interest that the Phillips curve has continued to arouse ever since its first appearance is indeed exceptional for such a short empirical study on political economy with relatively little theoretical content. After the publication of Phillips' contribution in *Economica* in 1958, the relationship between unemployment and wage changes was studied and discussed in a wide spectrum of analyses by economists from different schools who have been involved in the debate on macroeconomics and political economy from 1958 to the present.

In the opinion of several authors, the great fortune of the Phillips curve stems mainly from shortcomings in the neo-classical synthesis of Keynesian theory. As Phillips' analysis theorized a highly stable inverse relationship between unemployment and inflation, it was at once perceived as the 'missing link' in orthodox Keynesian thought which could explain the tendency of prices to rise slowly but constantly – a trend which was observed across boundaries in advanced capitalistic countries following World War II. And this is also the reason why the 'Phillips relationship' promptly generated a myriad of theoretical models and empirical estimates upon being first introduced into the synthesis model in the 1960s.

In the following decade the Phillips curve came in for severe criticism from monetarists because it was held to be a prominent element of orthodox thought in the 1960s. Friedman and other monetarists voiced criticisms both against the curve itself (including Lipsey's and other economists' approaches to the unemployment–inflation trade-off) and the political–economic strategy menus that was held to derive from it. And although the Keynesian interpretations that were proposed in those years, especially Tobin's (1972), were interesting in themselves, they obtained decidedly less consensus from professional economists.

Over the past decades Phillips' empirical result has also been variously interpreted by neo-classical theorists. As the interpretations proposed by the latter provide the main theoretical basis for the aggregate supply curve, it may be assumed that the debate on the unemployment–inflation relationship in progress in those years was mainly intended to explore the microfoundations of the aggregate supply function. The same can be said of the new classical macroeconomic approach, also named *mark II monetarism*, one of whose theoretical merits is to have carried Friedman's and Phelps' criticisms of the original Phillips curve to extremes.

The Phillips curve has also received attention from a number of neo-Keynesian, Kaleckian and Marxist thinkers whose interpretations of the unemployment–inflation relationship greatly diverge from neo-classical ones. Abandoning the postulate of a decreasing marginal productivity of labour, they have succeeded in reconciling Phillips' empirical finding more directly with Keynesian macroeconomic models.

In this book we will discuss the evolution of the debate on the Phillips curve with particular attention to non-neoclassical interpretations of the relationship between unemployment and inflation.

The first chapter examines Phillips' and Lipsey's contributions in detail and, following a discussion of the main conclusions of the debate in the '60s, expands upon Samuelsen's and Solow's theses on the Phillips curve as an 'economic policy menu'.

The second chapter discusses monetarist criticisms of the Phillips curve and Friedman's and Phelps' theory of the Natural Rate of Unemployment (NRU), paying some attention to two significant non-monetarist contributions published in the '70s, namely Tobin's 1972 article on 'Inflation and Unemployment' and Desai's writings which were put together in book form in 1981.

The third chapter presents the main neoclassical explanation of the Phillips curve, the job search theory, highlighting the theoretical foundations of the neoclassical interpretation of this celebrated curve as well as the criticisms that were levied against it in consequence of some barely realistic assumptions and by reference to the findings of empirical research.

The fourth chapter discusses re-elaborations of the Phillips curve that were suggested by some theorists of stagflation and illustrates the relationship between income policies and the unemployment–inflation trade-off.

The fifth chapter provides a detailed discussion of two heterodox models of the Phillips curve: the model suggested by Rowthorn, in which the relationship between unemployment, inflation and money is traced back to the conflict over the distribution of income between capitalists and workers, and a Kaleckian model in which the role of the social conflict over the unemployment–inflation trade-off is viewed from a different perspective.

The closing chapter of the book is entirely concerned with illustrating how the conflict between the various schools further evolved, passing from the opposition of NRU to NAIRU (non-accelerating inflation rate of unemployment) to the debate on the hysteresis of the NRU and on the existence of multiple equilibria.

The Phillips curve and its different interpretations are thus the leit-motif of the whole book, whose aim is to present a wide range of different theories which followed upon one another over the last 40 years during which the unemployment–inflation trade-off remained at the forefront of the debate in the fields of macroeconomics and political economy. Nonetheless the book does not attempt to present an exhaustive picture of the Phillips curve. Rather, holding non-neoclassical approaches to this celebrated curve to be far more realistic and thus more interesting, the authors have chosen to address this debate with a slight bias in favour of these interpretations. Consequently the chapters and sections in which the trade-off concerned is illustrated from a more orthodox perspective – i.e. by constantly explaining the working of the labour market in terms of the law of demand and supply, of a decreasing marginal productivity and increasing marginal substitutability of labour and free time – are not so much intended to make a thorough study of the huge range of analyses which fit into this interpretative approach, as to analyse in great depth the non-neoclassical theses concerning the inverse relationship between unemployment and inflation. As far as these are concerned, the authors have attempted to provide as complete a picture as possible. A heart felt thank you to Mrs Ambrosio for her precise and careful editing work.

1 The origins: Phillips' and Lipsey's contribution

1.1 INTRODUCTION

As mentioned in the Preface, in macroeconomic studies Phillips' contribution has been the object of much attention over the last forty years. It is therefore fitting that we analyse both Phillips' 1958 paper and the theoretical approaches to the unemployment–inflation trade-off that were propounded in the years immediately following its appearance.

First of all, in Section 1.2 of this chapter we will focus on the purpose of Phillips' article and clarify its findings. Very often works which receive great attention are re-examined time and again and the relevant re-interpretations give credit to the original even though its implications and objectives were not always correctly understood. An article published by Lipsey in 1960 certainly played an important role in the case of the Phillips curve. Lipsey's interpretation, which linked Phillips' contribution with Keynesian neoclassical synthesis, and the divisive debate this was found to ignite throughout the 1960s will be dealt with in Sections 1.3 to 1.6 of this chapter. At the same time we will also point out a number of shortcomings in Lipsey's theoretical contribution which were severely criticized by neoclassical economists in the subsequent period.

A paper published by Samuelson and Solow in 1960 greatly encouraged attempts to generalize Phillips' result. Besides testing the Phillips curve against the situation in the United States, these authors were the first to suggest that the Phillips curve could be viewed as an economic policy *menu*. Samuelson and Solow's paper and its implications are examined in Sections 1.7 and 1.8, while the last Section of this chapter contains a number of concluding reflections.

1.2 THE PHILLIPS CURVE

Phillips' article was published in *Economica* in February 1958. In an empirical study investigating the relations between percentage variations in wages and unemployment levels in the United Kingdom over roughly one century (1861–1957), this LSE economist pointed out a surprisingly regular trend which was especially noticeable in the first 52 years of that period (up to 1913). This seemed to suggest that each unemployment level is associated with a given rate of change in money wages and that the relevant relationship is so stable that by controlling aggregate demand, and hence employment, one can control both money wages and prices.

Phillips set out from the equation:

$$(\dot{w} + a) = bu^{-c} \tag{1.1}$$

where $\dot{w}$ is the growth rate of wages, u is the unemployment rate and a, b and c are three parameters. In logarithmic terms, (1.1) is written as follows:

$$\log(\dot{w} + a) = \log b - c \log u \tag{1.2}$$

Translating Phillips' analysis into graph form, let us assume that $\dot{w}$ on the ordinate is the rate of change in money wages and u on the abscissa is the rate of employment; by duly processing the figures available for the United Kingdom in the period 1861–1957, Phillips found that there was a non-linear inverse relationship (see Figure 1.1) between the growth rate of wages and unemployment levels.

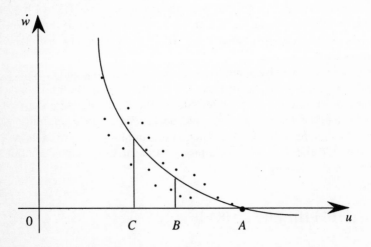

Figure 1.1   The Phillips curve

In the case under review, Phillips also found that:

a. there were unemployment rates at which money wages were seen to decrease; consequently he identified an unemployment level on the curve, approximately 5.5%, at which the wage level remained stable (which means that the Phillips curve intercepted the x-axis at a 5.5% rate of unemployment);
b. as the slope was steeper for lower unemployment levels, the curve was evidence that the growth rates in money wages rose very steeply as unemployment decreased;
c. there was a threshold value – about 1% of the working population throughout the period considered – below which unemployment could not fall;
d. not only unemployment levels, but also their *variations* were important when explaining changes in wage rates and price levels (this fact can be explained by bearing in mind that in periods of declining unemployment firms found it more difficult to hire new workers and were consequently willing to pay higher wages);
e. a negligible impact of the cost of living index on the growth rate of money wages was observed during periods in which the prices of imported goods did not rise steeply;

The novelty or importance of Phillips' result did not lie in his identification of an inverse functional relationship between unemployment levels and changes in money wages (since this relationship had been observed several times before, for example by Irving Fisher, Keynes and Marx),[1] but in his contention that this relationship was a *stable* one, because this meant that a given unemployment level would always generate the same rate of change in wages (for example, with unemployment at 2.5% the rate of change in money wages would constantly tend to be 2% both today and in the future, as it did 50 years ago).

Phillips provided only a few explanations of the empirical relationship he had discovered. It would appear that he interpreted his findings by stating that as the labour market, like every other market, was governed by the law of supply and demand, rises in wages at low unemployment levels were mainly due to the fact that when aggregate demand is high and the workforce shrinks, businessmen compete with one another by offering higher wages in order to attract workers from other firms or industries.[2] Two years later Lipsey continued his analysis further and propounded a more precise theoretical reconstruction of the trade-off discovered by Phillips.

1.3   LIPSEY'S INTERPRETATION OF THE PHILLIPS CURVE

Like Phillips himself, Lipsey also (see Lipsey, 1960) explained the famous curve in the context of the law of supply and demand, i.e. by arguing that money wages only rise when there is excess demand for labour, whereas they actually decrease when the supply of labour exceeds demand. It follows, therefore, that point A in Figure 1.1, i.e. the x-intercept of the Phillips curve at which money wages are stable, must be the point at which demand for labour equals supply and where the labour market is consequently in equilibrium. But equilibrium in the labour market does not necessarily mean that there is no unemployment. The Phillips curve itself points to a degree of unemployment (equal to 0A) at point A. In line with the job search theory, Lipsey explained this finding by arguing that, given the slow re-adjustment process, in each period there are workers in search of jobs on the one hand and vacancies on the other (since each worker has limited access to information and those who are looking for a job will not find one immediately despite the existence of vacancies). In Lipsey's interpretation, 0A is thus the level of *frictional* unemployment and corresponds to what Friedman and monetarists later termed the *natural* rate of unemployment (see Chapter 2).

Let us now consider a point to the left of A. Based on the above reflections, this must be a point at which demand for labour exceeds supply because it reflects a situation with vacancies exceeding the number of workers seeking employment. What will happen in such a situation?

It goes without saying that, the greater the gap between demand and supply of labour, and thus the greater the difference between the number of vacancies and the unemployment level, the easier it will be to find jobs and the more the unemployment level will decrease. However, according to the interpretation we are examining here, unemployment can *never be zero* because in a market economy there will always be workers wishing to switch from one job to another and/or young people seeking first time employment and because it does take time to find a job. From this it follows that in Lipsey's interpretation the Phillips curve can never touch the ordinate, but will continue to rise ever more steeply as unemployment decreases.

According to Lipsey, therefore, a low unemployment level sparks off a wage hike because it necessarily results in more vacancies compared to the number of jobless, so that firms will compete with one another to secure the few workers available in the market. And there is no denying that the more firms compete for workers available, the more wages will tend to increase.

Let us mention that when the relationship between rising wages and unemployment is explored in the light of this explanation it is far from easy to tell causes from effects, since disequilibrium arises in connection with the gap between demand for and supply of labour and readjustment can be obtained, or described, in the two different ways summed up here below:

a. when wage levels are stable, excess demand for labour reduces unemployment (because it facilitates job seeking) and the consequential decrease in unemployment rates pushes up wages;[3]
b. excess demand for labour boosts wages[4] and the rise in wages makes workers more inclined to accept the jobs they are offered; as a consequence, unemployment falls.

As will be shown further on, the later debate on the Phillips curve was often centred on this dual causal mechanism.

Lipsey also addressed the problem of *loops* – a finding which Phillips too had dealt with: as is confirmed by data evidence, wages tend to rise at a comparatively quicker pace during an expansionary phase and diminish at a comparatively quicker pace during periods of difficulty. As the points plotted for the data concerned move from point *b* on the curve to the left (owing to the upturn in economic activity), they will be located above the slope, whilst those further to the right (as a consequence of a downturn in economic activity) will be found below the curve; the result is an anticlockwise circular movement of the type shown in Figure 1.2. To explain this finding, Phillips argued that in periods of *falling* unemployment firms begin to realize that they have difficulty in finding workers; fearing that things will become even worse in future (i.e. as their expectations change), they rush to hire the workers they are able to find by offering more advantageous terms of employment than they would otherwise have done, whilst during *an upward movement* in unemployment they tend to do the opposite.[5] However, in his original article Phillips also argued that the steeper rise in wages observed at declining unemployment levels was due to the upward spiral in prices caused by an expansionary phase. Regardless of the explanation finally chosen, in Phillips' approach to these loops a wage hike is ultimately due not only to the employment rate as such, but also to *changes* in employment levels. This is the finding that emerged from his empirical study.

Phillips' interpretation of loops was criticised by Lipsey, who held it unreasonable to assume that the changing expectations of economic agents concerning future changes associated with a decreasing trend in unemployment in the labour market would induce employers to pay higher wages at each unemployment level (with the points rising above the curve), though not to hire more workers at each wage level (with the points moving down below the curve). Thus, assuming that each rise in unemployment boosts while reducing u, there is no means of establishing if, setting out from a point such as b, the points reflecting the future situation will be located above or below the Phillips curve (see Lipsey, 1960, pp. 20–1).

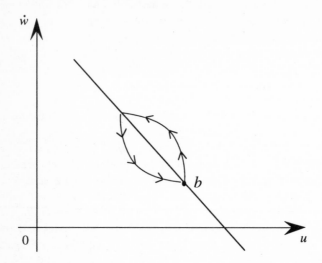

Figure 1.2   The loops

Deeming Phillips' interpretation of *loops* unacceptable, Lipsey propounded an alternative one. In his opinion the reason why the slope of the Phillips curve is pushed upward during expansionary phases is that unemployment is increasingly dispersed across labour markets. An expansionary trend, he argued, has a different impact on different markets, generating bottlenecks (in markets) where the rise in demand is highest and, consequently, a brisker boost in wage rates than would have been registered if that same unemployment rate had been more evenly distributed across the markets concerned; conversely, during periods of depression decreases in demand are more evenly distributed across industries. According to Lipsey, the result of this is that loops 'can be accounted for in an hypothesis that the recovery affects different markets at different times while the fall in effective demand is, at least during the early stage of the recession, more evenly distributed' (Lipsey, 1960, p. 23).

As will be shown further on, this interpretation of loops has also aroused both perplexities and open criticism (see Section 1.5 below).

1.4　A FORMAL ILLUSTRATION OF THE LIPSEY MODEL

Lipsey's approach will be better understood if his contribution is discussed in greater detail. Lipsey set out from the trend in a micro-labour market defined as one where the internal rate of change in unemployment exceeded the difference between its own unemployment levels and those of other markets (Jackman, Mulvey and Trevithick, 1981, pp. 33–53). According to Lipsey, sectorial changes in wage rates are due to excess demand registered within the sector itself. Consequently we can state:

$$\dot{w}_i = g\left(E_{di}\right) \qquad (i = 1, \dots, n) \qquad (1.3)$$

where the suffix i stands for one of n submarkets considered and Ed reflects excess demand. This can be defined as follows:

$$E_{di} = \frac{\left(N_{di} - N_{si}\right)}{N_{si}} \qquad (1.4)$$

where N stands for jobs and the suffixes d and s respectively stand for demand and supply.

Here demand for labour is to be interpreted as *planned* or *notional*[6] and consequently includes both jobs filled (N) and vacancies (V). Hence:

$$N_{di} = N_i + V_i \qquad (1.5)$$

Similarly, supply of labour is to be interpreted as planned and must consequently include both the employed and the jobless (U):

$$N_{si} = N_i + U_i \qquad (1.6)$$

Substituting (1.5) and (1.6) into (1.4), the result is:

$$E_{di} = \frac{\left(V_i - U_i\right)}{N_{si}} = v_i - u_i \qquad (1.7)$$

where $v = \dfrac{V}{N_s}$ and $u = \dfrac{U}{N_s}$ and, consequently:

$$E_{di} \geq 0 \quad \text{if} \quad v_i \geq u_i$$

Lipsey assumed that the unemployment level could be considered a proxy of the excess demand value, so that:

$$E_{di} = h(u_i) \qquad (1.8)$$

with the following properties:

$$h' < 0 \qquad h'' = 0 \qquad \text{if} \quad E_{di} \leq 0$$
$$h' < 0 \qquad h'' > 0 \qquad \text{if} \quad E_{di} > 0$$

Substituting (1.8) into (1.3), the result is:

$$\dot{w}_i = g\left[h(u_i)\right] \qquad (1.9)$$

which is the relationship discovered by Phillips.

The Phillips curve for a single market can be constructed in a graph with four quadrants (Figure 1.3).

The relationship (1.8) between excess demand and unemployment is represented in the first quadrant; the relationship (1.3) between the rate of change in wages and excess demand for labour is represented (in linear form) in the second quadrant; in the third quadrant the variable $\dot{w}$ is transferred onto the axis of ordinates and lastly the Phillips curve is plotted in the fourth quadrant.

From the above it follows that in Lipsey's interpretation the relationship between unemployment and the rise in wage rates is based on two assumptions:

a excess demand must be a proxy of the unemployment rate;
b. there must be a function reflecting the response of money wages to excess demand for labour.

All this is evidence that Lipsey considered the Phillips curve an empirical finding to be brought into line with the law of demand and supply and that he held inflation to be of the demand-pull type.

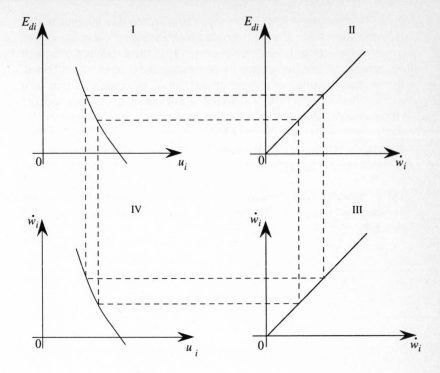

Figure 1.3   The Phillips curve of Lipsey

1.5   A CRITICAL ANALYSIS OF LIPSEY'S APPROACH

Leaving aside the problem of loops, let us now consider just any point on the curve, for example point *b* in Figure 1.4, and let us assume that a country experienced the situation reflected at that point over a number of successive years. How are we to interpret the situation in that country? And, in particular, how are we to account for the *stability* of a situation (the same unemployment rate and the same rate of change in wages over a number of years) which, being a condition of *disequilibrium*, one would have expected to be highly mutable?

From the perspective of the interpretation we are dealing with here, any change in money wages has, by its very nature, a balancing function and thus tends to eliminate excess demand for labour. If no such readjustment occurs and the situation reflected in point *b* (with *the same* excess demand

for labour continuing in time) is found to persist, this can only mean that
the demand curve has shifted to the right and/or the supply curve has moved
to the left to an extent barely sufficient to offset the balancing effects of
changes in $\dot{w}$, so that the amount of excess demand is in no way affected.

But such a situation can only be brought about by chance. In fact, as it
is reasonable to assume that the labour demand and supply curves undergo
constant change, shifts by exactly the measure required to keep excess
demand constant can only occur by sheer accident. As a result, in Lipsey's
interpretation it would by far from realistic to assume that such a situation,
i.e. a stable rate of change in wages, should persist in any country year after
year.

Let us now consider the case in which the situation in a country over
three subsequent years is reflected in the sequence of points b, c and d in
Figure 1.4.

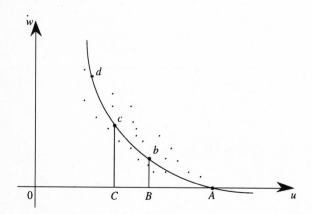

Figure 1.4   A critical analysis of Lipsey's approach

How can this sequence be explained? According to Lipsey it means that
shifts in the demand and/or supply curves have occurred in such a way as
to increase imbalance *despite* the rise in wage rates. However, this case
cannot be assumed to be the rule, given the tendency of changes in wage
rates to re-establish equilibrium in the labour market; nor is it realistic to
assume that – *as a rule* – shifts in labour demand and supply curves not only
cancel out such trends towards equilibrium, but actually tend to create ever
greater imbalances.

Thus the typical sequence for a country governed by Lipseyan style
mechanisms seems to be c, b, A, that is to say a sequence where imbalances
in the labour market decrease year after year.

This conclusion is not consistent with empirical findings. Indeed, if the above were true, the situations most often observed in reality would correspond to points lying around the equilibrium point *A* in Figure 4 and the data collected across countries would paint a scenario with labour markets in equilibrium, stable unemployment rates and equally stable wage rates provided that no increases in productivity are recorded. However, as a rule things do not work out like this.

Lipsey's interpretation of the Phillips curve also comes in for further criticism. As mentioned above, Lipsey contends that any increase in excess demand for labour reduces unemployment either because it eases the search for jobs or because, by boosting wages, it induces workers to accept available jobs more willingly. However, from the perfect competition perspective of neoclassical theory, any short-term rise in demand for labour must be interpreted as a move along the labour demand curve which does not transpose the demand curve as a whole. In point of fact the labour demand curve reflects the marginal productivity of labour and the latter, being determined by technology, is not subject to shifting as a result of changes in price levels. In particular, in the neoclassical perfect competition model any rise in aggregate demand for commodities, far from shifting the labour demand curve, produces a movement along the curve itself. Hence there is no reason to argue that an increase in aggregate demand for commodities should reduce unemployment on the part of the Phillips curve to the left of its x-axis intercept.

To illustrate this point in greater detail, let us trace an elementary graph with a variable on the abscissa reflecting the number of workers and a variable on the ordinate reflecting the real wage rate (the ratio of the money wage rate, w, to the general level of prices, p). Let L_D and L_S respectively be a labour demand curve and a labour supply curve (see Figure 1.5). Setting out from the equilibrium point E, where demand for and supply of labour are both equal to $0F$, any increase in demand for commodities will push up the price level, reduce the real wage rate and cause a rise in demand for labour (owing to a movement along the curve L_D) from $0F$, for example, to $0G$. At the lower wage rate, $0B$, labour supply will decline to $0H$ and, as a result, employment will also drop to $0H$ (because the cause which determines an increase in demand for labour will also determine a decline in labour supply).

Hence the conclusion that no movement along the Phillips curve to the left of the abscissa intercept can be assumed in a neoclassical model with perfect competition (see Phelps, 1970a, p. 2). As has been observed, the 'incorporation of Lipsey's theoretical concept of the Phillips curve in our macroeconomic model is incompatible with the neoclassical theory of labour supply' (Stevenson, Muscatelli and Gregory, 1988, p. 59). We will come back to this point later on to show how this obstacle was overcome in first and second generation monetarist literature.

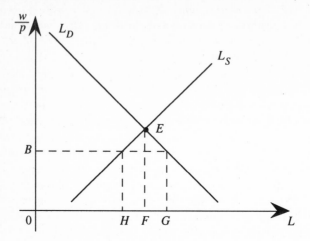

Figure 1.5   Equilibrium in the labor market and the Phillips curve

As for Lipsey's explanation of *loops*, objections to his thesis (increasing dispersion of unemployment across labour micro-markets in expansionary phases) include the fact that it is not supported by sufficient factual evidence (see Archibald, 1969) and the observation that especially after World War II the typical cycle was a loop with points plotted in a clockwise, and not anti-clockwise fashion (see Grossman, 1974). Among many alternative explanations of this phenomenon, the one propounded, in particular, by Hines centres around the idea that the unemployment rate is not a good proxy of excess demand in the labour market because in an expansionary phase a rise in demand creates more jobs than are actually filled (and thus excess demand for labour increases even further in connection with a fall in the unemployment rate). It follows, therefore, that in an expansionary phase the unemployment rate underestimates actual excess demand in the labour market and, if wages increase in proportion to such excess demand, at each successive unemployment level wages increase more steeply than one would have expected based on the Phillips curve. The reverse is observed in a period of depression (see Hines, 1971).

Let us add that some consider it far from realistic to assume, as Lipsey does, that the number of job seekers should remain constant when demand for labour and real wage levels are both on the increase. In their opinion it is the number of those leaving their jobs to search for better ones that increases during a wage hike; and this means that in a period of rising wage rates unemployment can either fall, increase or remain stable and that a *rising* or vertical Phillips curve is consequently possible (see Corry and Laidler, 1967, pp. 194–5). In the next section we will show that this criticism has been put into the right perspective (see Vanderkamp, 1968).

Although the question of the procedure Phillips initially adopted in plotting his curve[7] will only be addressed in passing in Section 6, the fact remains that Lipsey's article was written in part with intent to criticize Phillips' 'bizarre way' of tackling statistical problems[8] and that the criticisms of Phillips' procedure voiced by several authors are for the greater part held to be pertinent and well grounded.

1.6   FURTHER CONSIDERATIONS ON LIPSEY'S INTERPRETATION OF THE PHILLIPS CURVE

To some of the above-mentioned criticisms Lipsey replied himself. [9] The arguments he set forth in support of his own approach will be better understood if we duly examine the model he presented in his 1974 article (see Lipsey, 1974).

Let us assume that there is no Walrasian auctioneer and that exchanges are consequently not made at equilibrium prices; as taught by disequilibrium theory, in such a situation the quantities exchanged depend on the 'short side', i.e. on whichever, demand or supply, is smaller. Moreover, let f be the percentage rate by which demand for labour exceeds supply, i.e. the difference between demand for and supply of labour expressed as a percentage:

$$\phi = \frac{N_D - N_S}{N_S} \tag{1.10}$$

Before we discuss Lipsey's interpretation, we have to explore the relationship between excess demand for labour and unemployment, which will be termed the $f - u$ relation.

In the absence of job searching (or frictional) unemployment, the unemployment level is zero when N_S is less than or equal to N_D, so that the $f - u$ relation can be illustrated in graph form in Figure 1.6 – where the employment rate has been marked on the abscissa and excess demand for labour, f (as a per cent rate), on the ordinate – with the piecewise-linear setting out from a, rising toward the origin of the axes and then coinciding with the ordinate. Conversely, in the presence of frictional unemployment the employment level will never be reflected either in the number of those looking for jobs or in the number of vacancies available; it will always remain below the smaller of these two values because there will always be firms seeking to fill their vacancies with suitable workers.

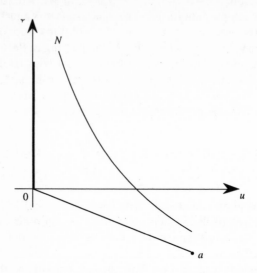

Figure 1.6   Unemployment and excess of the demand for labour

In this case the relationship assumes the shape of the N-curve in Figure 1.6. At this point let us assume that those seeking jobs in the period commencing today, called the newly unemployed NU, are a constant percentage of those, E, who are currently employed, so that:

$$NU = \alpha E \qquad\qquad (1.11)$$

and let us also assume, as is usual in job search theory (see Chapter 3), that the number of those newly employed (NE), i.e. of those who find a job in the period starting from today, increases in proportion to the number of jobs available and in proportion to those in search of a job. As the number of positions firms are trying to fill by hiring suitable workers, called V, equals the difference between total available jobs, J, and jobs filled, E, and only the unemployed, U, are assumed to be in search of jobs, if, for the sake of simplicity, we assume that those who find a job (the newly employed) are a constant proportion, β, of the product V by U, we have:

$$NE = \beta VU = \beta(J-E)U \qquad\qquad (1.12)$$

Bearing in mind that unemployment is stable when the flow of those who leave their jobs equals the flow of those who find a new job and that consequently an unemployment level satisfying the $NU = NE$ condition can be termed *equilibrium unemployment*, the result is:

$$\frac{dU}{dt} = NU - NE = \alpha E - \beta (J - E) U \qquad (1.13)$$

and, in an equilibrium situation, when $\dfrac{dU}{dt} = 0$

$$\alpha E = \beta (J - E) U \qquad (1.14)$$

As, by definition:

$$L_S = E + U \qquad (1.15)$$

reorganizing (1.14), one obtains:

$$\alpha (L_S - U) = \beta (J - L_S + U) U \qquad (1.16)$$

and, therefore:

$$\alpha \frac{L_S}{U} - \alpha = \beta (J - L_S + U) \qquad (1.17)$$

from which:

$$J = -\frac{\alpha}{\beta} - U + L_S + \frac{\alpha}{\beta} \frac{L_S}{U} \qquad (1.18)$$

As demand for labour, J, depends on the wage rate, w, if L_S is assumed to be stable, (1.18) proves to be a simple relationship between w and U and can consequently be used to trace a Phillips curve.

To develop and enhance the analysis while continuing to use linear relationships, let us now assume that:

$$NU = aE + bV - cU \qquad (1.19)$$

that is to say that the number of job seekers increases in proportion to the number of those currently employed and the number of vacancies, but decreases inversely to those unemployed. These assumptions are plausible because it is reasonable to think that the more jobs are vacant and the smaller the number of people already in search of a job, the greater the number of those who will start searching for jobs. Let us also assume that:

$$NE = dU + eV \tag{1.20}$$

and let the positive constant e be greater than the positive constant b of formula (1.19), which means that the influence of vacancies is greater on NE than on NU. These assumptions are also plausible because on the one hand it is reasonable to assume that the number of those who find a job is proportional both to the number of those looking for jobs and the number of vacancies, whilst on the other it is obvious that the effect of vacancies on NE is generally greater than that on NU.

As vacancies are, by definition:

$$V = L_D - (L_S - U) \tag{1.21}$$

substituting (1.17) and (1.21) into (1.19) and (1.20), one obtains:

$$NU = aL_S + b(L_D - L_S) - (a - b + c)U \tag{1.22}$$

$$NE = (d + e)U + e(L_D - L_S) \tag{1.23}$$

Bearing in mind that equilibrium unemployment is the situation in which $NU = NE$, solving (1.22) and (1.23) for U we obtain the following result:

$$U_E = \frac{aL_S + (b - e)(L_D - L_S)}{a - b + c + d + e}$$

and, dividing by L_S, we obtain:

$$\frac{U_E}{L_S} = u = \frac{a + (b - e)\phi}{a - b + c + d + e} \tag{1.24}$$

where, as mentioned before, $\phi = L_D/L_S - 1$. Bearing in mind that $e > b$, from (1.24) it follows that:

$$\frac{du}{d\phi} = \frac{b - e}{a - b + c + d + e} < 0$$

And this is evidence that, contrary to the opinion expressed by Corry and Laidler, Hines and Holmes and Smyth in opposition to Lipsey's 1960 article[10], the relationship $\phi - u$ can be plotted as a decreasing curve. Therefore:

– *unemployment decreases whenever demand increases or supply of labour diminishes.*[11]

Adding the obvious but fundamental Lipsey relationship according to which the rate of change in wage rates ($\dot{w}$) increases in proportion to the increase in excess demand for labour, we can proceed from the $\phi - u$ relationship to the $\dot{w} - u$ relationship of the Phillips curve, which is again illustrated in Figure 1.7.

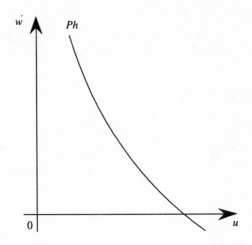

Figure 1.7   *The Phillips curve*

At this point we will ascertain if unemployment actually moves toward its equilibrium level as indicated by equation (1.24). As is inferred from (1.22) and (1.23), the value of *NE* increases in proportion to unemployment, while the value of *NU* can either increase or decrease; but as we set out from the assumption that $e > b$ and as we know that d, c and a are positive constants, we can easily conclude that:

$$(d + e) > (b - c - a)$$

which determines that even when *NU* increases in proportion to *U*, it will rise less than *NE*; consequently the possible shapes of the curves that reflect (1.22) and (1.23) for given values of L_D and L_S are those plotted in Figures 1.8 and 1.9.

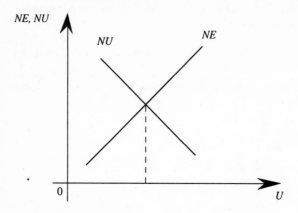

Figure 1.8   The NE and NU curves

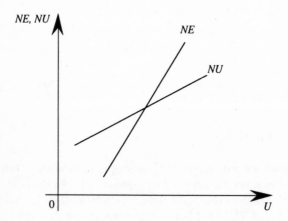

Figure 1.9   The NE and NU curves

Thus, so long as unemployment remains below the equilibrium level *NU* will be greater than *NE* in the situations presented in both these figures, with unemployment increasing in line with (1.13); and vice versa.

Consequently the system will tend toward equilibrium unemployment, i.e. toward the intercept of the Phillips curve on the x-axis.

Yet this situation is open to the criticisms that were expounded on pp. 10–12 above.

1.7   A GENERALIZATION OF PHILLIPS' RESULTS

Two years after the publication of Phillips' paper, Samuelson and Solow wrote an essay to demonstrate that the relationship pointed out by Phillips for the United Kingdom was also applicable to the United States (see Samuelson and Solow, 1960; as well as Bhatia, 1962, among the earliest studies); later on a wealth of empirical studies published up until 1967 or so showed that the Phillips curve was also applicable to other countries (see, for example, Kaliski, 1964).[12] These empirical studies and the implications drawn from Lipsey's interpretation (which we intend to illustrate further on) gave great credit to the Phillips curve.

Samuelson and Solow were the first to argue that the Phillips' curve could throw light on the relationship between inflation and unemployment. This result can be directly inferred from Phillips' relationship:

$$\dot{w}_t = f(u_t) \qquad \text{with } f' < 0 \ \ f'' > 0 \quad (1.25)$$

assuming that the rate of change of the general price level is always equal to the difference between the growth rate of money wages and the growth rate of the productivity of labour:

$$\dot{p}_t = \dot{w}_t - \dot{\pi}_t \tag{1.26}$$

In this case, if the growth rates of wages and prices are both marked on the ordinate, below each Phillips curve *PH* (which reflects the growth rates of wages at successive unemployment levels) we can plot an additional curve, *Ph*, which reflects the rates of change in prices corresponding to single unemployment levels (see Figure 1.10); and if the growth rate of labour productivity is constant, i.e. independent of employment levels, the vertical distance between the two curves is also constant, which means that the two curves are parallel to each other.

Needless to say, *Ph* curves can be equated with Phillips curves to all intents and purposes and, given the close link between these two types of curves, any observation made with reference to *PH* can easily be applied to the *Ph* curves.

Samuelson and Solow did not note any substantial dissimilarities between the Phillips curves for the United Kingdom and the United States in the period 1900–20. For the years 1946–58 they found that wages in the United States remained stable at an 8% unemployment level and rose by 2.5% – the average labour productivity increase – when unemployment stood at approx. 6%. In more general terms they found that the Phillips curve for the United States was steeper and was located much further to the right than that for the United Kingdom. In the opinion of Samuelson and Solow this was due to the fact that long periods of high employment, growing price levels and equally high trade union membership rates among the working population had resulted in greater wage growth rates in the United States than in the United Kingdom although both countries had the same unemployment rates.

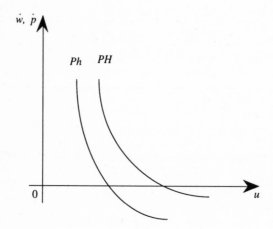

Figure 1.10   The Phillips curve of Samuelson and Solow

Part of the interest aroused by the Phillips curve was due to two far-reaching corollaries that were derived from it. The first of these, which was implicit in Lipsey's thesis that changes in wage levels too were governed by the law of supply and demand, involved a vindication of the superiority of economics over politics, i.e. the finding that trade unions and workers would have no say in determining wage levels if the relationship reflected in the Phillips curve was actually as rigorous and stable as its author had maintained and had long been assumed.

The second corollary of the Phillips curve concerns inflation and is the contention that the only means of preventing rises in wage levels from determining price increases is to reduce aggregate demand and (consequently) employment – which is tantamount to saying that monetary stabilization can only be achieved by accepting a certain amount of unemployment. According to mainstream opinion in the 1960s the Phillips curve obliged society to make precise economic policy choices in terms of a suitable trade-off between unemployment and inflation. Society can afford a lower rate of inflation, even one near zero, provided it is prepared to pay a price – in terms of unemployment and excess capacity – sufficiently high to keep check on prices and wages.[13]

Another reason which may explain why the Phillips curve was regarded as an important instrument of analysis is that it threw light on the fact that full employment is not an obstacle which appears out of the blue, almost as if there was a clear-cut distinction between unemployment and shortage of labour; on the contrary, there is a large area in which any change in employment adds to inflationary pressure not only because of decreasing production capacity, but also because of greater difficulties in finding fresh manpower. This, too, gave further credit to this celebrated curve because it was in line with a creeping inflationary trend underway in many advanced capitalistic economies in the late 1950s and early 1960s.

1.8   THE PHILLIPS CURVE AS AN ECONOMIC POLICY MENU

As mentioned in the previous section, Samuelson and Solow also defined the Phillips curve as being a sort of *economic policy menu*. They held that this relationship presented politicians with a list of different trade-offs to choose from between inflation and unemployment (see Samuelson and Solow, 1960, pp. 187–94 and Rees, 1970). In point of fact, the stability observed by Phillips in the case of the United Kingdom and by other researchers in other countries as well seemed to suggest that policy makers could choose a specific inflation–unemployment combination by controlling aggregate demand. Even though this contributed to blur the full-employment goal, the most immediate economic policy objective following World War II (see, for instance, the Beveridge Report in Great Britain, Beveridge, 1944), the Phillips curve clearly pointed to the possibility of choosing the preferred unemployment–inflation trade-off.

Soon the conviction spread that the action of a government could be assessed in political terms based on whatever point on the Phillips curve it chose: as a rule, a government opting for a point with low unemployment and high inflation is left-wing (because it is leftist parties that usually defend the interests of workers and tend to reduce unemployment even at the cost of a rise in inflation),[14] while a government opting for a point with low inflation and high unemployment is probably *right-wing*, because it is the right that shows greater concern with the disorder and reduction in the value of savings that inflation entails.[15]

According to many authors, this argument has been proved wrong in countries with two-party systems. Following a pioneer study by Downs (see Downs, 1957, which in turn joins up with a classical paper by Hotelling, 1929), mainstream opinion has it (and historical experience confirms) that the two parties tend to converge and become, as it were, an ideal half-way house between the far right and the far left (because a party veering away from the middle of the road would lose votes to the benefit of the other). In other words, according to Downs a party aiming to win an election in a two-party system has no choice between different policies and there is always only one policy which proves to be the most expedient choice in every situation.

Down's thesis has repeatedly come in for severe criticism (see, for instance, Kramer, 1977) on account of its highly restrictive assumptions (e.g. for assuming that both the electorate and the government are perfectly informed, postulating symmetrical positions for government and opposition and, most importantly, ignoring the fact that power is in the hands of the government). Setting out from less restrictive hypotheses, Nordhaus used the Phillips curve to demonstrate the existence of a precise political cycle: having won an election, a government initially tends to bring about an increase in unemployment and then lets it gradually decline until the following general election, so that the inflation rate falls sharply immediately after the election and then starts rising continuously until the next one (see Nordhaus, 1975). However, the Nordhaus model has also been the object of much criticism (see Frey and Schneider, 1978; McCallum, 1977 and Kirschgassner, 1984).

To some extent the recent literature which presents the Phillips curve as a prerequisite that policy makers are required to meet when choosing the economic policy menu they deem best suited to maximize collective welfare[16] ties in with this debate.

1.9   CONCLUSION

Reconstructing the early debate on the Phillips curve we emphasized the scope it offered for tracing the empirical 1958 result back to the Keynesian synthesis paradigm; as is well known, this holds that the labour market mechanism is very similar to that of other markets although characteristics such as wage rigidity and informational friction prevent price mechanisms from balancing out demand and supply in every situation.

The shortcomings of this reconstruction are basically two: firstly, none of the traditional explanations of wage rigidity are compatible with the neo-classical postulates concerning the rational behaviour of *homo oeconomicus*; secondly, informational problems have not been adequately addressed.

In later years these shortcomings were tackled according to two different approaches.

The traditional neoclassical approach brought Phillips' empirical results and theorizations into line with the neoclassical logic of demand for and supply of labour. The relevant theories will be discussed in the following two chapters.

Conversely, the labour-market mechanism behind the explanations of the Phillips curve suggested by heterodox theorists was entirely unrelated to the logic of supply and demand. In the last three chapters of this book we will analyse and discuss a number of contributions which stem from this non-neoclassical perspective.

NOTES

1. See Fisher, 1926, p. 496ff. Keynes (1936, p. 301) points out the existence of 'semi-critical points at which an increasing effective demand tends to raise money wages'. In some well-known pages of *Capital* Marx had linked the growth of money wages to the 'reserve industrial army' (see Marx, 1867, pp. 781–94). Also Dicks-Mireaux, Dow, 1959, reached similar findings simultaneously with and independently of Phillips. See also Klein and Ball, 1959.

2. Phillips explicitly stated that his work was based on the assumption that wage rates rise because employers compete with one another in order to secure workers and that the findings of his empirical research confirmed the assumption that wages usually rise in a 'demand pull' labour market: 'When the demand for labour is high and there are very few unemployed we should expect employers to bid wage rates up quite rapidly, each firm and each industry being continually tempted to offer a little above the prevailing rates to attract the most suitable labor from other firms and industries' (Phillips, 1958, p. 283). None the less he seemed to be convinced that it was the unemployment level that influenced the inflation rate (as maintained by advocates of the cost-push inflation theory), and not vice versa (i.e. that it was not the inflation rate that influenced unemployment levels), as is usually held by the majority of those who explain the Phillips curve with excess demand in the labour market (see Phillips, 1958, pp. 284 and 298 and,

      among others, Nevile, 1979, p. 111). It was for this reason that he came in for severe criticism from Friedman.

3. Lipsey's interpretation of the Phillips curve – Corry and Laidler wrote – 'it is the level of unemployment that "determines" the rate of change in wages, $\dot{w}$ rather than the reverse' (see Corry and Laidler, 1967, p. 190).

4. This is usually considered to be the 'basic adjustment hypothesis' of Lipsey's interpretation (see Vanderkamp, 1968, pp. 179 and 183; Corry and Laidler, 1967).

5. In Phillips' own words, 'in a year of rising business activity, with the demand for labour increasing and the percentage unemployment decreasing, employers will be bidding more vigorously for the services of labour than they would be in a year during which the percentage unemployment was the same but the demand for labour was not increasing' (Phillips, 1958, p. 283).

6. Here the term *notional* is used in line with the definition given in disequilibrium literature, see Clower, 1965. For further information, see Frisch, 1983, pp. 36–41.

7. Routh is one of the authors who found fault with the quality of Phillips' data. Discussing matters concerning the statistical material used by the English economist, he pointed out many imperfections (and argued that by remedying them one would reach findings utterly different from Phillips'; see Routh, 1959). However, Phillips' results were recently confirmed in a reflection on Phillips' econometric study by Wulwick, 1996, pp. 393–409.

8. For these criticisms, see Santomero and Seater, 1978, pp. 501–2.

9. This problem was first raised in Corry and Laidler, 1967. See also Fischer, 1988, pp. 26–8.

10. See Corry and Laidler, 1967, pp. 194–6; Hines, 1971, pp. 143–8; Holmes and Smyth, 1970, pp. 311–5. As a result of these criticisms it was assumed that unemployment was not a satisfactory proxy of excess demand in the labour market; hence the proposal that the latter was to be measured using the additional data on vacancies as well (see Dicks-Mireaux and Dow, 1959 and Hansen, 1970).

11. The relationship expressed by (1.20) is linear as a consequence of the assumptions behind it, though it is reasonable to assume that the value of e, which reflects the relationship between the number of those who find jobs and the number of vacancies, decreases at any increase in vacancies. But as the number of vacancies is driven up by any increase in ϕ, e is a decreasing function of ϕ, which means that higher the level of ϕ the value of u is found to decrease, as shown by curve N in Figure 1.6.

12. Appraisals of empirical analyses of the Phillips curve can be found in Santomero and Seater, 1978, pp. 513–4 and Jackman, Mulvey and Trevitick, 1981, pp. 50–62.

13. Solow, 1977, pp. 50–60. In this connection, arguing openly against those who held the Phillips curve to be an improvement on Keynesian theory, Weintraub wrote: 'If unemployment is the answer to the inflation issue, then Keynesianism as a social philosophy is dead; literally interred by Keynesians themselves and, curiously, all in the name of the mentor' (see Weintraub, 1960, p. 154).

14. As forcibly argued by Hutchinson, in the 1950s and 1960s it was Keynesian mainstream thinkers (Kahn, Robinson and Harrod), not Keynes himself, that held the view that British unemployment levels were too high at that time. Especially in the last years of his life Keynes himself appeared to be much more concerned about inflation (see Hutchinson, 1977).

15. However, as long as exchange rates are fixed (as they were until 1973), this remains a purely theoretical approach to the issue. In a fixed exchange rate regime, a country opting for a precise point on the Phillips curve resulting in higher inflation levels than those prevailing in the rest of the world was in fact subject to recurring balance of payment crises (because firms lost competitiveness on world markets) and was consequently obliged to resort to repeated currency devaluation or to adopt disinflation strategies. In point of fact, this is one reason why the trade-off afforded by the Phillips curve was held to be an argument for the adoption of a flexible rate system (see, for example, Johnson, 1972 and Argy, 1981).

16. Most of the relevant literature fits within the New Classical Macroeconomics (NCM) movement and originated from a well-known paper by Kydland and Prescott (1977).

2 Keynesians and Monetarists on the Phillips curve

2.1 INTRODUCTION

As mentioned before, the Phillips curve soon became 'the missing link' in Keynesian theory and, very likely for this reason, the main target against which monetarists aimed their criticisms. To understand the first issue, it will be useful to ask ourselves why Phillips' 1958 paper met with such great success, since the answer to this question may suggest a number of interesting reflections concerning the Keynesian nature of the initial interpretations of the Phillips curve.

The reasons underlying the success of Phillips' 1958 essay have intrigued all those who have analysed Phillips' trade-off, leaving them wondering why such a short and not particularly rigorous contribution which was not entirely original (we have already mentioned contributions by Fisher (1926), Dicks-Mireaux, Dow (1959), and Klein, Ball (1959)), was so successful as to feature in the debates on macroeconomics and political economy for more than 30 years.

Analysing the debate on the unemployment–inflation trade-off in the first 20 years after the publication of the paper, in 1978 Santomero and Seater came up with three explanations for the success of the Phillips curve (see Santomero and Seater, 1978, p. 500):

> First, Phillips's article appeared a few months earlier than others; second, Phillips's article was extended in a brilliant piece by Richard Lipsey; third, and probably most important, only Phillips drew the eye-catching, now famous curve that bears his name.

Disagreeing with Santomero and Seater, other academics suggested that the success of the paper was mainly due to the fact that its findings could easily be integrated into the neoclassical synthesis model of Keynesian economics and made to fill the main 'gap' of that theoretical paradigm. Indeed, the Phillips curve made it possible to investigate the labour market more thoroughly and appropriately than Hicks and Modigliani had done moving within the Keynesian tradition. As mentioned before, by general agreement the latter had only addressed the issue of the rigidity of money wages.

In the same year, 1978, Lipsey, too wrote:

> The Curve provided a theoretical link between the Keynesian IS-LM macromodel and labour markets. This link made it unnecessary to assume rigid money wages in order to make the Keynesian macromodel work. The labour market was effectively integrated into the Keynesian model and the stage was set for a fuller study of how this link operates (Lipsey, 1978, p. 55).

And this idea of Lipsey's certainly obtained wide consensus within the academic world.

The integration of the Phillips curve into the *IS-LM* model and the improvement upon its usual interpretation afforded by a more exacting analysis of the labour market itself and its impact on overall macroeconomic equilibrium also provided a fresh opportunity to explain inflation, a phenomenon which the paradigm of the neoclassical synthesis of Keynesian theory had so far been *unable to explain* because of the use of a fixed price model. Desai's opinion on this point (see Desai, 1981, p. 59) can be of some interest here:

> [The Phillips curve] seemed to most economists in the early sixties to provide the missing element in the Keynesian model. Now there was a theory of inflation which could be integrated into the IS-LM framework and the Keynesian edifice was completed (Desai, 1981, p. 59).

On closer analysis, however, the different propositions reported above are not mutually exclusive; thus it is possible to conclude that Santomero and Seater's and Lipsey's and Desai's interpretations can be drawn together. It follows, therefore, that on the one hand the success of the 1958 paper can be traced back to marginal factors – for instance the graphic representation of the empirical findings – and, on the other, it can also be explained by the fact that the Phillips curve fits in with the dominant model of the time to the point of becoming the basic component of a theoretical model capable of explaining economic occurrences more thoroughly.

The above reflections may also support the second statement made at the beginning of this section; i.e. the contention that the Phillips curve, which was held to be part of the Keynesian model that Friedman and other monetarists intended to call into question, soon became one of the main targets of monetarist attacks on the dominant orthodox theory of the time.

In this chapter we are going to discuss in detail the monetarists' criticisms of the Phillips curve (Sections 2.2–2.5) and the interpretation of the unemployment–inflation trade-off from the perspective of new classical macroeconomics (Section 2.6). Two Sections (2.7–2.8) are concerned with heterodox interpretations of the Phillips curve which challenged monetarist criticisms by reproposing the idea of an inverse relationship between unemployment and inflation and Section 2.9 presents a few concluding observations.

2.2   FRIEDMAN'S AND PHELPS' CRITICISMS OF THE PHILLIPS CURVE

The monetarists' criticisms of the Phillips curve can be discussed by setting out from their reinterpretation of the concept of 'full employment':[1] if unemployment is a situation in which people are searching for jobs and if a certain amount of frictional unemployment is registered at all times (because, they held, there are always some people seeking work), then 'full employment' must be termed the situation in which *demand* for labour from employers wishing to fill their job vacancies is exactly matched by *supply* of labour, i.e. by the number of those unemployed; if this is true, they argue, it would be better to revise the dominant technical jargon and, accepting the fact that a certain unemployment rate is a matter of course, term 'natural rate of unemployment' the rate at which demand for labour equals supply for labour and the labour market is substantially in equilibrium (with the wage rate remaining roughly constant) because the number of vacancies equals the number of those unemployed.

It is worth noting that the importance of this definition stems from the fact that by its very nature the natural rate of unemployment is determined solely by real (not monetary) factors such as the standard of living of the population, the degree of market viscosity and the extent of unemployment relief (which variously affects labour supply) (see Friedman, 1968, p.8 and Haltiwanger, 1987, p. 610). However, the adjective 'natural' must not be taken to suggest that this rate is either constant or determined by long-lasting forces, for in actual fact every time one of the decisive real factors is found to change (for instance if the income tax rate is increased), the natural rate also changes (because, in the example given before, higher income taxes may prove to be an inducement to work less).

Bearing in mind the above, monetarists argue that as the natural rate of unemployment is an exclusively real phenomenon, monetary phenomena such as an increase in money supply or an expected general rise in inflation cannot permanently subvert this equilibrium level of unemployment in the long run.

For a graphic illustration of this (see Figure 2.1), let us trace a Phillips curve *PH* assuming that the current and expected inflation rate is given and constant and that 0*F is the natural rate of unemployment*; according to Lipsey's interpretation, if the level of production is seen to increase following a rise in global demand, then money wages would also have to increase and unemployment would have to decline from *F* to *A*. However, based on the observations Phelps and Friedman made before any others, this will only be true in the short run, because in the long run (given that an increase in wages boosts prices) expectations concerning prices will have to be revised and this will cause a steeper rise in money wages at each unemployment level. This means that the *PH* curve will continuously be shifted upward until these expectations are 'corrected'. Bearing in mind that by definition long-term equilibrium excludes wrong forecasts, on the new Phillips curve *PH'* the equilibrium point will proceed from *F* to *F'* and prices and wages will rise, year after year, by the rate *FF'* (assuming that there will be no increases in productivity). But in the opinion of monetarists this means that as long as real factors remain constant, the long-term Phillips curve is a vertical line, PH_L, which intersects the abscissa in *F*.

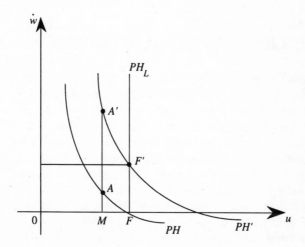

Figure 2.1　Monetarism and Phillips curve

The distinction between expected and unexpected actions, which is at the root of what has been said above, has acquired great prominence in contemporary economic theory, since it appeared obvious that explaining an inflationary trend which never occurred in the past is one thing, whilst explaining an inflationary trend which was actually experienced in the past and is consequently anticipated both by firms and workers is another; and it stands to the merit of monetarists to have greatly emphasized the importance of expectations in explaining inflation.

The explanation of inflation based on expectations has been gaining ever greater credit ever since, in the 1960s, prices and wages began to increase much more rapidly than would have been expected based on the original interpretation of the Phillips curve, thus providing factual evidence of the instability of short-term curves and showing beyond any doubt that the Phillips curves, provided they do exist, are continually shifted upward as prices rise. In other words, the theory of expectations explains why, after some time, prices are likely to rise more than a single Phillips curve would make us expect. But there are some who suggested that the Phillips curve tends to remain stable as long as the inflation rate does not exceed a given value (assumed to be around 4 or 4.5%), but becomes unstable when the inflation rate rises more steeply.

To understand this we must clarify the procedure with which monetarists reconstruct the short-term Phillips curve and the role played by expectations.

2.3   A MONETARIST INTERPRETATION OF THE PHILLIPS CURVE IN THE SHORT RUN

According to Friedman, Phillips made a major mistake when he established a relationship between a real value (u) and a monetary value ($\dot{w}$); for, if it is true that individuals are mainly concerned with real values, it is clear that the relation between a real and a merely monetary value can be valid at best in the short run, i.e. during an adjustment phase, but not in the long run.

In Friedman's opinion the problem discussed by Phillips had already been properly dealt with in an essay by I. Fisher (see Fisher, 1926). By further developing Fisher's analysis, Friedman explains the relationship between inflation and unemployment as follows (see Friedman, 1975). Let us assume that for some reason the level of global demand is found to increase and that, consequently, increases are registered both in prices and in money wages. Initially, as long as expectations on future prices do not change or, better still, until consumers realize that prices have increased everywhere, workers will interpret the rise in money wages as an increase in real wages and will consequently offer more work; as long as employers fail to realize that price levels have been on the increase everywhere, they will in turn interpret the boost in the prices of their products as a change to their benefit in relative prices.

From the perspective of the labour market, the situation described by Friedman is one in which the labour supply curve will be shifted (see Figure 2.2). As workers are under a monetary illusion, the labour supply curve will be shifted to the left as a result of the rise in money wages and prices and workers will be prepared to offer a greater amount of work although the real wage rate has in no way increased. If firms, too, are prey to this monetary illusion (that is, if they focus on the rise in the prices of their products without being aware of the general price rise), the labour demand curve will also move to the right. However, as Friedman failed to suggest this occurrence, the curve N_D can be left in its original position. Thus the graph in Figure 2.2 uncovers the apparent mystery surrounding the direct relationship between increasing wages and employment in the Phillips curve: in actual fact this relation is only produced by monetary illusion, for as soon as we focus on real values the rise in employment is found to be accompanied by a *fall* in real wages from 0A *to* 0B (as shown in Figure 2.2) and not by a rise (as one might wrongly assume looking at the Phillips curve).

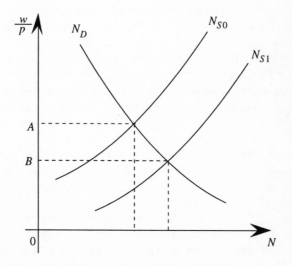

Figure 2.2   Monetarism and labour market equilibrium

On closer analysis, the reflections developed above also suggest a different causal link from the one assumed by Phillips, since employment increases *as a result* of the price and wage increases, and not vice versa.[2] But what will happen in the long run?

2.4   THE PHILLIPS CURVE IN THE LONG RUN

The above reflections, or rather the arguments which hold the position of
the Phillips curve to be determined by the *expected* rise in prices, encouraged
the plotting of an *expectation augmented* Phillips curve. The idea, which
today is widely accepted, is that there is a Phillips curve for each expected
price increase and that any change in expectations causes a shift in the
Phillips curve.

Consequently the monetarists' equation for the Phillips curve can be
written as follows:

$$\dot{w}_t = f(u) + \dot{p}_t^e \qquad\qquad (2.1)$$

where $\dot{p}_t^e$ is the expected rate of increase in prices for the period t. From the
expression (2.2) it clearly follows that the Phillips curve will change
position depending on the level of expectations from time to time.

Let us mark again the unemployment rate, u, on the abscissa and the rate
of increase in prices and wages on the ordinate (see Figure 2.3). Given the
rate of increase in prices at time 0, the Phillips curve that can be plotted for
the short term will have the usual slope. An example of this is the curve
Ph_0, which intersects the abscissa at point E. At the expected rate of
increase in inflation wages will begin to rise more rapidly and the Phillips
curve will be shifted upward, so that at time 1 it will be, let us say, in
position Ph_1. Let us now assume that the Ph_0 curve has been plotted based
on the assumption that on the outset the rate of increase in prices is
expected to be $\dot{p}_t^e = 0$ and that the curve Ph_1 is plotted based on the
assumption that the rate of increase in prices expected for time 1 is $\dot{p}_t^e$,
which is greater than zero. When the expected rate of inflation is zero, in
E the actual rate of increase in prices is also zero and therefore equal to the
expected rate of increase. Provided no change occurs, this situation will
last in time. If, conversely, an expansionary policy tends to reduce
unemployment, there will be an initial movement along Ph_0, for example
from E to A, where the actual rate of increase in prices is $\dot{p}_1$, i.e. greater than
the expected rate. This poses the following problem: can the situation
reflected at point A last in time?

It is apparent that the situation at point A cannot be stable because at A
the actual rate of increase in prices is greater than the expected rate of
increase and this will induce a revision in the relevant expectations. Let us
now consider the simplest case of adaptive expectations, the one whereby
the inflation rate expected for time t is always the rate that was actually
registered in the period before; in this case, some time later, as time

progresses from 0 to 1, the *expectation augmented* Phillips curve will move from position Ph_0 to position Ph_1 and consequently the state of the economy can no longer be reflected by point A. How will the situation evolve?

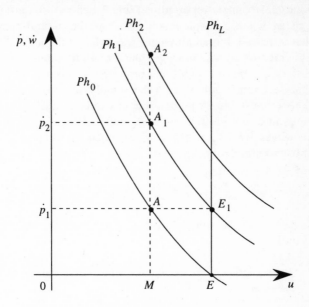

Figure 2.3   The Phillips curve in the long-run

Let us consider two different cases. In the first case the government takes action as soon as the inflationary spiral starts rising and promptly reduces global demand to its previous level at time 0; unemployment falls back to level $0E$ and, with the new Phillips curve Ph_1, the actual rate of increase in the price level is $\dot{p}_1$, as was expected. Thus E_1 is the new equilibrium position where employment is again equal to $0E$, whilst the level of inflation has progressed to rate EE_1 – a position of stable equilibrium since the actual inflation rate equals the rate that had been expected.

In the second case the government, having reduced unemployment to level $0M$ and obtained an inflation rate as low as $\dot{p}_1$, insists on keeping global demand high in order to stabilize unemployment at the new level. In this event the economy will proceed at first from position A to position A_1 because when the expected rate of inflation is $\dot{p}_1$ and the Phillips curve is Ph_1, unemployment will only remain stable at $0M$ if inflation is left to soar to the rate MA_1. However, A_1 will not be a stable position either, because the Phillips curve will again be shifted upward, to Ph_2, as soon as the inflation rate reaches p_2 and when this occurs unemployment will only remain stable at $0M$ if the inflation rate is allowed to reach a rate equal to MA_2; and so on.[3]

The numerical example reported in Table 2.1 shows that inflation will continue rising when unemployment is below the natural rate. Let us assume that in period 0 unemployment was 6%, i.e. the natural rate, and that both the rate of increase in wages and the inflation rate were 0. What will the rate of increase in wages and prices be in subsequent years if an expansionary economic policy reduces unemployment to 5% in period 1 and keeps this rate stable throughout the next four years?

If, as a result of the Phillips relation, the initial fall in unemployment pushes up wages by 2%, and if it is assumed that expectations arise according to this simple mechanism:

$$\dot{p}_t^e = \dot{p}_{t-1} = \dot{w}_{t-1} \qquad (2.2)$$

considering (2.1), in the subsequent four periods wages and prices will increase as follows:

Table 2.1   *The reduction of the unemployment and acceleration of the inflation*

Period	u	$f(u)$	$\dot{p}_t^e$ (%)	$\dot{w}_t = \dot{p}_t$ (%)
0	6	0	0	0
1	5	2	0	2
2	5	2	2	4
3	5	2	4	6
4	5	2	6	8
5	5	2	8	10

What has been said above has important implications in terms of political economy, since based on the graph in Figure 2.3 a government wishing to reduce unemployment to a value below $0E$, for instance to $0M$, will have to let inflation rise steadily year after year. Furthermore, even though a rise in demand shifting the equilibrium point from E to A were to determine, in due time, a shift back from A to E_1, where prices and wages increase at the rate EE_1, an attempt to bring the rate of unemployment back to $0M$ would cause a movement along the new short-period curve Ph_1 and the rate of change in prices and wages would be MA_1, which is greater than MA; and so on. This implies that in the long run there is no trade-off between inflation and unemployment.

In analytical terms, the equation of the Phillips curve is as follows:

$$\dot{w}_t = f(u - u_n) + \dot{p}_t^e \qquad \text{with } f'(u - u_n) < 0 \quad \text{and} \quad f(0) = 0 \quad (2.3)$$

where u_n is the natural rate of unemployment.

Considering the previous equation (2.2), the result is:

$$\dot{w} = \dot{w}_{t-1} \qquad \qquad \text{if, and only if} \quad u = u_n \qquad \qquad (2.4)$$

In the long run this implies that the Phillips curve will be a vertical line parallel to the ordinate, since only when unemployment reaches its natural rate will the system achieve equilibrium and preserve it in subsequent periods as well.

Concluding, we can say that according to monetarists 'today's Phillips curve may be largely inherited but tomorrow's curve will depend upon how the economy behaves today' – 'in such a way, to be precise, that steady inflation will not "buy" a permanent (non-vanishing) reduction of the unemployment rate' (Phelps, 1969, p. 148).

2.5 THE NATURAL RATE OF UNEMPLOYMENT AND THE INEFFECTIVENESS OF ECONOMIC POLICY

The natural rate of unemployment is both one of the crucial points of the monetarists' theoretical construction and one of the main points of their radical criticisms of Keynesian economic thought. Friedman, who introduced the concept, defined it at times as the rate of unemployment at which no Keynesian 'involuntary' unemployment is registered, but at other times as the rate of unemployment at which anticipated inflation is matched by the actual rate of inflation, regardless of whether such unemployment as is registered at that rate is voluntary or involuntary.

In his celebrated 1968 paper on monetary policy Friedman defined the natural rate of unemployment as:

> the level that would be ground out by the Walrasian system of general equilibrium equations, provided there is embedded in them the actual structural characteristics of the labor and commodity markets, including market imperfections, stochastic variability in demands and supplies, the costs of mobility and so on (Friedman, 1968, p. 8).

and many economists felt that his definition actually reflected a level of unemployment corresponding to full employment. In the 1970s, therefore, the monetarist interpretation of the Phillips curve and of the natural rate of unemployment was often presented (based on the definition printed above) as an up-to-date version of the neoclassical theory according to which the economic system constantly tends towards full employment equilibrium: i.e. the point at which, assuming zero-inflation expectations, the traditional Phillips curve intersects the abscissa at a level of unemployment corresponding to full employment.[4]

Evidence of the foregoing is provided by a large number of writings published in the 1970s in which the natural rate of unemployment was interpreted in this manner and, above all, by Friedman's coeval contributions: in a famous 1975 essay, for instance, upon presenting a graph combining demand and supply of labour with a Phillips curve, Friedman explicitly argued that the point at which the Phillips curve intersects the abscissa is the equilibrium point of demand and supply of labour and that there:

> Unemployment is zero – which is to say, as measured, equal to 'frictional' or 'transitional' unemployment, or, to use the terminology I adopted some years ago from Wicksell, at its 'natural rate' (Friedman, 1975, now in Friedman, 1990, p. 66).

In contrast with Friedman's own arguments, however, the different definitions he proposed are found to diverge greatly. Owing to the observations on the shortcomings of markets and lack of information he set forth in a 1968 paper, his interpretation of the 'natural rate' can be viewed as an updated approach to full employment only if all the unemployment that 'arises from the actions made by workers individually or collectively, in particular through unions', is defined as voluntary (Malinvaud, 1984, p. 29); in his 1968 paper, Friedman himself admitted:

> It is worth noting that this 'natural' rate need not correspond to equality between the number of unemployed and the number of job vacancies. For any given structure of labor market, there will be some equilibrium relation between these two magnitudes, but there is no reason why it should be one of equality (Friedman, 1968, p. 8, fn 3).

In Friedman's definitions of the 1970s the natural rate of unemployment was interpreted in such a way as to coincide with Beveridge's idea of full employment, according to which workers are fully employed when the number of vacant jobs equals the number of those unemployed, as in the quotes reported above (since it is obvious that unemployment is zero when demand for labour equals supply and that demand for and supply of labour coincide when the number of those unemployed equals the number of vacant jobs).

The problem of the correct interpretation of Friedman's concept of the natural unemployment rate and the criticisms it came in for will be addressed in greater detail in a different section (see, in particular, Section 6.2); here it will be sufficient to ask ourselves why the existence of a natural rate makes it impossible to boost production and employment levels using the usual levers available to control aggregate demand, i.e. why it implies a criticism of Keynesian views concerning economic policy.

Let us assume that the current situation is reflected in point A and is characterized by the natural rate of unemployment and by zero-inflation, and let us also assume that the government should opt for expansionary policies which cause the unemployment rate to fall back from 0A to 0B (see Figure 2.3); based on the reflections developed in the previous paragraphs, this will only be feasible in the short run, because the system would soon move on to point C and, failing further economic policy moves, remain stable there. It is worth noting that in point C the rate of unemployment is again 0A, while the rate of change in wages (and prices) is no longer zero, as it was in the starting situation, but equal to AC, a value which tends to be restored in subsequent periods. This implies that any attempt by the government to reduce unemployment would not only prove ephemeral but would even ignite inflationary pressures which, far from 'cooling down' as a matter of course, would tend to reappear in subsequent periods at least until restrictive policies reverse expectations.

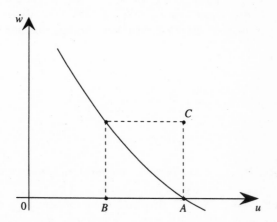

Figure 2.4   The natural rate of unemployment

In conclusion, the trade-off theorized by Phillips is entirely dependent on the stability of the curve which is named after him and loses any validity

under the severe criticisms of monetarists. From the perspective of
Friedman, Phelps and other monetarists there is only one level of output
and employment that the economy can assume and any attempt to force the
economy into a different kind of equilibrium will not only be ineffectual,
but will even spark off an inflationary spiral which only restrictive economic
policies will halt.

2.6   NEW CLASSICAL MACROECONOMICS AND THE PHILLIPS CURVE

New classical macroeconomics has taken the monetarists' criticisms of the
Phillips curve to extremes. Although monetarists disputed the effects of the
inverse relationship between unemployment and inflation on economic
policy, they did not go so far as to deny the short-term trade off straightaway.
They simply argued that a temporary reduction in unemployment could
only be obtained at the cost of continually rising prices, while a permanent
halt to unemployment would imply having to put up with an ongoing
inflationary trend. Taking these criticisms of the Phillips curve even
further, new classical macroeconomics has definitively disproved the
assumption that policy makers have any option between inflation and
unemployment even in the short run.

In support of what has just been said it may be useful to draw an
extremely simplified macroeconomic model[5] and then solve it by recourse
to the method proposed for solving models with rational expectations:

$$\dot{m}_t = \dot{p}_t + \dot{x}_t \qquad (2.5)$$

$$\dot{p}_t = g\left(\dot{x}_t - \dot{x}_t^*\right) + E\left(\frac{\dot{p}_t}{I_{t-1}}\right) \qquad (2.6)$$

$$\dot{m}_t = \dot{m}_t^* + \varepsilon_t \qquad (2.7)$$

where the last term expresses expectations concerning the inflation level at
time t based on the information available at time $t - 1$.

Equation (2.5) is the quantitative equation in its dynamic form; here it
represents the global demand equation. Equation (2.6) is a Phillips curve
equation in which the term that reflects unemployment has been replaced
with one reflecting the deviation of the rate of change in production from
its 'natural' value x^*; obviously it is also the aggregate supply curve of this
simple model. Equation (2.7) expresses the Central Bank's economic

policy rule with which economic agents are assumed to be conversant; $\dot{m}_t^*$ is the deterministic component of the increase in money supply, while ε_t is the corresponding stochastic component and is assumed to be symmetrically distributed in such a way that its average value is zero.[6]

Let us mention, at this point, that to identify the Phillips curve with the aggregate supply curve is equal to arguing that output and employment vary in accordance with the price level determined by voluntary choices made by individuals within markets assumed to be constantly in equilibrium; and this means that unemployment arises from the inability of markets to transmit correct information, not to bring buyers and sellers together and make their respective choices compatible.

As can be seen, the model is 'complete in itself'. Within this approach, it is in fact impossible to discuss the Phillips curve out of its context. Indeed, as operators 'put to good use' any information available, the moment when rational expectations are introduced only a macroeconomic model describing the economic system as a whole will afford making predictions concerning the trend in inflation.

The first step to be taken when determining inflation levels and output growth is to solve the system of equations (2.5–2.7) by assuming that expectations are still exogenous.[7] The result is:

$$\dot{x}_t = \frac{g}{1+g}\dot{x}^* + \frac{1}{1+g}\left(\dot{m}^* + \varepsilon_t - E\dot{p}_t\right) \tag{2.8}$$

where $E\dot{p}_t$ reflects expectations concerning the price level.

The second step is to calculate the value of setting out from the model as a whole and writing the set of equations (2.5–2.7) in its *expected form*:

$$E\left(\dot{m}_t\right) = E\left(\dot{p}_t\right) + E\left(\dot{x}_t\right) \tag{2.5 bis}$$

$$E\left(\dot{p}_t\right) = gE\left(\dot{x}_t - \dot{x}_t^*\right) + E\left(\frac{\dot{p}_t}{I_{t-1}}\right) \tag{2.6 bis}$$

$$E\left(\dot{m}_t\right) = E\left(\dot{m}_t^*\right) \tag{2.7 bis}$$

where E is the symbol standing for expectations.

Once the required substitutions and simplifications have been made, we obtain:

$$E\left(\dot{p}_t\right) = \dot{m}_t^* - \dot{x}^* \tag{2.9}$$

At this point equation (2.9) can be substituted into equation (2.8) and the third and last step for the solution of this simple New Classical Macroeconomics model can be taken:

$$\dot{x}_t = \dot{x}^* + \frac{1}{1+g}\varepsilon_t \qquad (2.10)$$

With respect to the rate of inflation, the same procedure leads to the following finding:

$$\dot{p} = \dot{m}^* - \dot{x}^* + \frac{g}{1+g}\varepsilon_t \qquad (2.11)$$

From (2.10) and (2.11) it clearly follows that the deterministic component of the rate of increase in money supply has no effect on output but only on inflation. Only the stochastic component of money supply, ε_t, can produce real effects, because its growth could not be 'anticipated' by economic operators.

Even in the short term, therefore, an expected increase in money supply will neither affect output nor employment. And this is why NCM theorists assume the short-term Phillips curve to be vertical or, better still, this is the reason why in a short-term perspective unemployment and inflation can proceed in opposite directions provided there is a 'surprise effect'.

In support of the above theses, Lucas and others brought empirical evidence showing that the trade-off concerned involves a 'greater cost' in countries with highly varying inflationary rates: in the opinion of new classical macroeconomists the favourable results of active aggregate demand policies are due to the fact that policy makers manage to take economic agents by surprise and this is more difficult in countries with higher inflation rates.[8]

2.7   TOBIN'S CRITICISM OF THE NRU HYPOTHESIS

A Keynesian answer to the monetarist NRU theory which also effectively criticizes monetarist (and NCM) propositions concerning the Phillips curve is found in a 1972 paper where Tobin explains the declining trend of the curve, its concavity and the difference between a full employment point and the curve's intercept on the abscissa in simple but highly effective terms. The arguments Tobin set forth in 1972 have been further corroborated by recent Keynesian studies on wage rigidity (see Akerlof, Dickens and Perry, 1996).

Following in Keynes' footsteps, Tobin attaches great importance to the downward rigidity of wages and consequently argues that excess demand for labour pushes wages up more steeply than an equal amount of excess supply of labour would cause them to fall. In his own words, 'unemployment retards money wages less than vacancies accelerate them' (Tobin, 1972, p. 10) because a more or less marked downward rigidity of wages results in *asymmetrical* movements in the labour market. This asymmetrical behaviour of wages determines a concave trend of the Phillips curve because any successive reduction in unemployment results in ever greater increases in the inflation rate, whereas when unemployment is at a high level any further rise produces a constantly smaller drop in the wage hike rate (see also Leeson, 1997).

To clarify this point, Tobin (like Lipsey) started by subdividing the aggregate labour market into a number of individual markets. A typical or normal situation, he argued, is one where excess demand is registered in some individual markets and excess supply in others. Even when the aggregate labour market is at its equilibrium level, there is no reason to assume that all individual markets should also be in balance: global labour demand and global labour supply are in equilibrium when any excess demand for labour in the markets with a shortage of labour is exactly matched by the excess supply of labour in those where labour supply exceeds demand. Thus it is possible to argue that whenever there is unemployment in the aggregate labour market the excess supply of labour registered in some markets exceeds the excess demand registered in others, while in the opposite situation an excess demand for labour in the aggregate market is a situation in which markets with excess demand prevail over those with excess supply of labour.

Combining together the two reflections discussed so far – the asymmetrical movements in wage levels and the imbalances in individual labour markets even when the aggregate labour market is in equilibrium – it is easy to find a plausible explanation for two closely interconnected issues which acquire prominence from the perspective of a Keynesian interpretation of the Phillips curve:

a. the concave profile of the Phillips curve;
b. the fact that its intercept on the abscissa does not coincide with the full employment unemployment rate.

As for the concave profile of the curve, from what has been said above it follows that the Phillips curve will never touch either the ordinate or the abscissa; it will never touch the ordinate because in a market economy, where there are always at least a few people switching over from one job to a better one (or young people who have so far been unable to find a first job suiting his/her qualifications), unemployment can never be zero; and it will never touch the abscissa (or will be the asymptote of a line parallel to it) because owing to the downward rigidity of money wages the Phillips curve evens out as unemployment increases.

What has been said so far can also throw light on the second issue. The downward rigidity of wages implies that in each individual labour market wages rise as soon as demand exceeds supply, but start declining only when unemployment exceeds a given threshold level. This implies that in situations of macroeconomic equilibrium between labour supply and labour demand, any rise in wages in markets with excess demand will not be offset by a fall in those with excess supply of labour. But this determines that when unemployment is at its equilibrium level (or natural rate, as monetarists would say), wages (or prices) are not stable, but rising, and that wage (or price) stability will only be achieved when unemployment rises above the level at which excess demand in some markets is exactly matched by excess supply in others.

It goes without saying that Tobin's argument is also applicable to monetarist expectation augmented Phillips curve models, in which the stability of real wages (defined as the situation in which) can only be reached when unemployment exceeds the rate at which excess supply in some labour markets is offset by excess demand in others.

In Tobin's analysis, therefore, the unemployment rate at which the Phillips curve intersects the abscissa is above the natural rate and is the rate, called NIRU (Non Inflationary Rate of Unemployment) or NAIRU (*Non-Accelerating Inflation Rate of Unemployment*), at which the level of involuntary unemployment is such that it neither accelerates nor slows down inflation: 'zero-inflation unemployment is not wholly voluntary, not optimal, I might even say not natural' (Tobin, 1972b, p. 216).

2.8   DESAI'S INTERPRETATION

The monetarist interpretation of the Phillips curve and the entire tradition of economic study which joins up with Lipsey's contribution were heavily criticized by Desai in several contributions. According to this economist from the London School of Economics the debate on the Phillips curve had taken a decidedly wrong turn for two reasons (see Desai, 1981, pp. 55–60):

1. 'distorting' both the original theoretical bases and the econometric procedure, Lipsey shifted emphasis toward the search for a short-term relationship which would account for those factors which drove up

wages in each year, while Phillips' aim was to find an approximate long-period relationship between wage increases and unemployment only;
2. in the USA, the authoritative voices of Solow and Samuelson launched the Phillips curve as an important tool of public policy, thus completing the metamorphosis of the curve within the span of two years from its first appearance.

Desai's arguments are best discussed starting from the econometric procedure adopted by Phillips. As mentioned before, Phillips chose the functional form:

$$(\dot{w} + a) = bu^{-c} \tag{2.12}$$

and estimated the corresponding linear transformation:

$$\log(\dot{w} + a) = \log b - c \log u \tag{2.13}$$

However, due to objective difficulties and, according to Desai, for other reasons as well, Phillips chose a decidedly odd procedure. Firstly, one obstacle was that only two of the three required parameters could be estimated using (2.13) and Phillips side-stepped it by initially setting $a = 0$. Secondly, Phillips had to determine the sum of the logarithms of the empirical values of and about half the figures he had available gave values equal to or below zero, i.e. values which have no logarithms. Thus he divided his set of data into six groups based on the following intervals measured on the abscissa: 0-2; 2-3; 3-4; 4-5; 5-7; 7-11 (with the upper limit comprised in each interval) and for each group he calculated the mean values of u and thus obtaining six pairs of values for the two variables. To estimate b and c he used the four of these pairs for which he had obtained a positive value of $\dot{w}$. Then he adjusted the function using the trial and error method and tried to obtain a value of a at which the curve would be as close as possible to the coordinates of the two pairs for which he had obtained a negative value of $\dot{w}$.

In Desai's view the numerous severe criticisms raised against Phillips' econometric procedure were due to a basic misinterpretation of his real aims. According to him, Phillips had provided sufficient and clear information on both the theoretical model behind the curve and the assumptions under which his analysis was valid. More precisely, he had clarified the following three points:

1. as mentioned above, in an *equilibrium* situation the price of labour responds in various ways to excess demand: when unemployment is

low, firms compete with one another to secure the few workers available and thus push up wages; when unemployment is high, as there is a minimum threshold below which workers would withdraw their services, wages become rigid with respect to unemployment. All this makes us assume that the relationship between $\dot{w}$ and u is decisively non-linear, as is expressed by (2.12);

2. in a non-equilibrium situation the fact that firms continue to offer higher wages can be explained by the cyclical influence of changes in demand for labour, and consequently of unemployment – an influence which is both symmetric and linear;

3. firms adjust (rather than fix) prices based on a weighted average of the variations registered in the cost of factors; thus they do not consider the prices of factors as given.

What Phillips set out to estimate was thus a structural relationship between $\dot{w}$ and u on condition that $\dot{u} = 0$ – a case which has never occurred in reality, but is none the less important to establish the long-term relationship between u and $\dot{w}$ from a theoretical perspective. The bizarre division into intervals and the subsequent calculation of means from the statistical data available were intended to extrapolate values purged of the *cycle* – a procedure which was made possible by the regularity of economic cycles in the period analysed by Phillips.

If this, as Desai maintains, is the correct interpretation, also the loops are to be viewed from a different perspective, i.e. they turn out to reflect fluctuations in economic cycles and could explain why the real values deviate from those estimated for the case in which $\dot{u} = 0$.

Desai's reconstruction of the Phillips curve has been termed 'ingenious and important' by Mark Gersovitz (1980, p. 439). If nothing else, it provides a different interpretation of an empirical study which had been all too hastily criticized by many. And although Desai's analysis has never received much credit in the theoretical and empirical re-elaborations, including *policy* debates, that Phillips' original contribution sparked off, it may be of some value in that it criticized the monetarists' theoretical propositions and suggested a different interpretation of Phillips' results.

2.9   CONCLUSION

The monetarists' criticisms of the Phillips curve – which were the subject of the opening sections of this chapter – played a decisive role in the debate over economic theory and political issues that started in the '70s: the concept of a natural rate of unemployment and the assumption that demand-management policies were ineffectual made rapid headway within the academic debate and the re-interpretations of the Phillips curve suggested by Keynesians in the '70s had little or no impact on the political strategies the governments of many Western countries were devising. It was not until the '90s that the notion of a natural rate of unemployment was superseded and that the effectiveness of Keynesian political approaches to the solution of the unemployment issue gained fresh impetus.

NOTES

1. Among the articles in which the criticisms of the Phillips curve reported below were first voiced, Friedman, 1968 and Phelps, 1970b are most often quoted. Actually the earliest paper in which Friedman denied the unemployment–inflation trade-off was Friedman, 1966 and the earliest contribution in which Phelps described the Phillips curve as outdated and immobile was Phelps, 1967.
2. In a 1977 paper by Modigliani, the attempt to reverse the causal relationship between inflation and unemployment which had emerged from the interpretations of the Phillips curve at that time was traced back to Friedman's 1968 article (see Modigliani, 1977, p. 5).
3. It is possible to show that this adjustment process may assume a cyclic pattern (see Argy, 1981, chapter xii) and data evidence is available to demonstrate that this adjustment process may go on for long periods of time (see Modigliani, 1977 and Tobin, 1980b).
4. In many manuals, the natural rate has continued to be defined in this fashion to this day; see, for example, Dornbusch and Fischer, 1994, p. 208 and pp. 505–06; Hall and Taylor, 1988, p. 368–69.
5. This model can also be considered a simplified version of the one proposed in Sargent and Wallace, 1976, pp. 153-70. On the role of rational expectations in the new classical macroeconomics approach, see Miller, 1994.
6. The choice of a simple fixed rule *à la* Friedman is not crucial to the results that will be obtained. As was recently emphasized in a debate on rules versus discretion (McCallum, 1996, pp. 215–23), the result in terms of the effectiveness of monetary policy would be the same even if (2.3) were written in the form of a *feedback rule*.
7. Concerning the procedure for solving models with rational expectations, see, for example, Sheffrin, 1983, pp. 40–6 and Minford and Peel, 1983.
8. See Lucas, 1973. For a different interpretation of this empirical evidence, see Ball, Mankiw and Romer, 1988.

3 Neoclassical interpretations of the Phillips curve and the microfoundations of macroeconomics

3.1 INTRODUCTION

As mentioned in the previous chapter, monetarists criticized both the unemployment–inflation trade-off that emerged from the Phillips curve and its alleged implications in terms of economic policy, while the greater part of the numerous neoclassical analyses of this celebrated curve were aimed to explain the short-term finding of an inverse relationship between rises in money wages and unemployment. As is well known, at first sight Phillips' findings are in contrast with the first postulate of neoclassical theory, according to which real wages match the decreasing marginal productivity of labour only when there is a direct relationship between unemployment and wages. Very often the attempt to reconcile Phillips' findings with neoclassical theory has involved substituting the perfect information assumption with that of asymmetric information, since this makes a direct relationship between wages (prices) and employment (production) possible in the short term. The most successful of the attempts to introduce the asymmetric information assumption into the models in question was doubtlessly Phelps' so-called 'parable of the islands' (see Section 3.2). This chapter is mainly concerned with discussing this parable and its use in connection with the construction of *job search* models (Sections 3.3–3.7).

All these theories sparked off a debate which is known as the analysis of the *microfoundations of macroeconomics* and experienced an extraordinary heyday in the 1970s and 1980s. In Section 3.8 we will try to set forth a few conclusions on the issues raised.

3.2 THE ASYMMETRIC INFORMATION ASSUMPTION AND PHELPS' PARABLE OF THE ISLANDS

We can start our analysis of the microeconomic foundations of the Phillips curve by stressing that the 1970s witnessed an entire set of (basically neoclassical) theories which read Phillips' finding as a relationship in which price rises (i.e. inflation) are the cause and rises in the quantity of commodities offered (and therefore employment) are the effect: a rise in prices pushes up employment and output levels through mechanisms which will now be outlined in detail, but which do not greatly differ from those already discussed in our analysis of the monetarist interpretation of the Phillips curve.

These mechanisms are best explained based on Phelps' so-called 'parable of the islands', a brilliant enunciation of the idea of 'asymmetric' information and a central component of all recent macroeconomic theorizations. According to this, economic agents are only assumed to be conversant with the price, or prices, of 'their own' market and not with prices prevailing elsewhere. As gathering information is costly, it is reasonable to assume that each individual is aware of what is happening in his/her immediate surrounding, i.e. in his/her own island, but not of what is going on in far-off places (in other 'islands'). Workers, in particular, would like to earn the highest real wages possible, but have difficulty in obtaining the information they need to establish what wage rate and what work conditions different firms would be prepared to offer. Only by inquiring near and far and stating their qualifications would they be able to obtain the required information, but this would entail leaving their current workplaces for several days and running the risk of being fired. Given these obstacles, it is again reasonable to assume that they too are well-informed of wages and prices in their firms, but have a very approximate knowledge of wages and prices in other firms. The latter, in turn, would find it in their interests to hire workers whose abilities and qualifications would suit those required for the business conducted by them. But since the costs involved in finding suitable workers are quite substantial, it is once again reasonable to assume that they know their own prices and the wages they themselves pay while ignoring prices and wages prevailing elsewhere.

This 'asymmetric' information assumption is useful in solving difficulties which arise in connection with the neoclassical approach to the construction of an aggregate supply curve due to the apparently direct relationship between wages and employment. Let us assume that in a situation of full employment prices are on the decline (as a result of a drop in demand). What will happen? As we know, demand for labour depends on the prices at which firms sell their products (because the higher the prices, the more firms will wish to boost their output and sales), but the decisive element is relative prices, i.e. the price level of one firm as compared to those of other firms. As mentioned before, when prices fall unexpectedly and information is asymmetric, every firm will be perfectly aware of the fall in the prices of its own products, but not of the decreasing prices of other products (in far-off 'islands'). Thinking that the relative prices of the articles it markets have diminished, the firm will be induced to offer fewer goods and thus to hire fewer workers. As for the latter, they are known to be concerned with real wages, but when wages and prices fall unexpectedly and the information they have available is imperfect, they will notice the lower wages they are being offered by the firm, but not the fall in the prices of goods; thinking it is their real wages that have decreased, they will tend to work less. In the case outlined above, the fall in prices and wages will thus reduce both supply and demand for labour, with a consequential fall both in employment and in aggregate supply.

In the situations described above the fall in employment can be traced back to imperfect information: as soon as firms and workers realize that their perceptions were imperfect, they will go back on their original decisions, so that in our example the fall in employment and supply levels is due to the so-called *surprise* effect, i.e. to the fact that asymmetric information causes incorrect perceptions in firms and workers.

In the opinion of Phelps, one of the first to develop this new interpretative approach, it is consequently useful to imagine the economic system as a set of islands in which information is retrieved at a cost (see Phelps, 1969, pp. 149–50) and in which economic agents always have available insufficient or wrong information.

In the above example adjustments in the labour market are caused by quantitative variations (in employment levels), not by price (i.e. wage) variations, because economic agents receive incorrect information on prices and revise their offer (in terms of labour and/or commodities) based on such wrong data. No fall in wages, but a decline in employment levels will be observed in the event a fall in aggregate demand produces excess supply of labour in the initial period. For the sake of completeness let us mention that the above reflections are based on the hypothesis that a worker intending to switch over to a different job is obliged to resign from his/her previous job (in order to have time to make the necessary inquiries – see below, Section 3.7).

Thus Phelps as well as others, including Alchian, concur with the Keynesian idea of a downward rigidity of money wages although they view it within a neoclassical context with voluntary unemployment. In their opinion unemployment stems from the fact that in situations of imperfect information money wages and prices take longer to adjust to changes in employment and production levels. What causes unemployment is lack of information, whilst in a Walrasian perfect-information context full employment would always be guaranteed by the instantaneous flexibility of wages and prices.

Thus the conclusion of these economists is that unemployment is always voluntary. We will come back to this point later on. For the time being it will be convenient to argue that the *surprise effect* is one of the weak points of the theory we are analysing here. In a world where mass media circulate information rapidly, to think that individuals faced with an unexpected increase or fall of prices and wages should still think (as they did in the past) that the change is confined to prices they are conversant with and to assume them making the same mistake time and again and being 'surprised' when their perceptions are again proved wrong in the circumstances of each case is indeed to take an unrealistic view.[1] Concerning this model Chrystal asked himself 'Why should a seller perceive the demand price for the product earlier than perceiving the general price level? It is quite possible that the reverse would be true. Aggregate information and forecast are much more widely available than information on specific market' (see Chrystal and Price, 1994, p. 63).

Furthermore, as workers and their families buy a variety of commodities of all kinds and often shop at short intervals between one purchase and the next, they would soon notice changes in the prices of commodities. Lastly, if it is true – as would seem from the perspective we are analysing – that upturns in the economy are always accompanied by rising prices, consumers would soon learn the lesson and, faced with a fresh *boom*, would notice that periods of booming economy are accompanied by rising prices, and vice versa.

The idea of Friedman, Phelps and others that a crisis always takes workers 'by surprise' and that falls in demand for labour would always result in a smaller quantity of labour being offered (because according to them workers notice that they are being offered lower wages but not that prices also are declining) is thus decisively unrealistic (see, for example, Gordon, 1981, p. 189).

3.3   AN INTRODUCTION TO THE JOB SEARCH THEORY

The *job search theory* originated from two well-known papers by Friedman and Alchian (see Friedman, 1968; Alchian, 1970) and was very much in vogue until some time ago. As will be shown further on, however, it is comparatively unrealistic and is perhaps applicable only to countries with a high mobility of labour such as the United States.

The foundations of the *job search theory* are markedly neoclassical, since two of its assumptions are a highly competitive labour market and the idea that in a situation of equilibrium real wages must be exactly matched by the marginal productivity and marginal disutility of labour. However, things are different in situations of disequilibrium or imperfect, wrong or insufficient information, which are exactly the ones to which Alchian, Phelps and many others have drawn attention.

The job search theory assumes that the labour market continuously tends towards full employment and that unemployment is, as a rule, *voluntary*. More precisely, its main tenet is that unemployment is usually 'frictional', i.e. arising from:

a. the fact that those dissatisfied with their work positions tend to leave their jobs in order to look for better ones;
b. the fact that those looking for first jobs or trying to switch over to better jobs take time to find satisfactory positions and in the meantime are out of work.

As this theory sets out from an analysis of the reasons why single workers are out of work, it can be termed a *microeconomic* theory of unemployment. In this context it clearly departs from the Keynesian idea that unemployment should be investigated considering the working of the economic system as a whole, not by generalizing the behaviours of single individuals which are responsible for single cases of unemployment.

The theory we are discussing sets out from the assumptions that:

a. there is a *natural rate of unemployment* at which demand for and supply of labour are equal;
b. the labour market, being comparable to a competitive market, works in such a way that wages fall every time supply exceeds demand for labour and are seen to increase when there is excess demand for labour; but the neoclassical nature of this theory is also inherent in the acceptance of the idea that any decrease in wages causes a decrease in unemployment, and vice versa.

According to this theory, job searching is a rational activity governed by precise cost/benefit calculations, whereby job seekers weigh the costs of their search against its benefits. As mentioned before, most analyses set out from the assumption that only those unemployed are seeking jobs because the search for a position requires much time and only those out of work can afford the time needed to conduct this search; consequently, in a situation in which only a limited body of information is usually available, the problem faced by job seekers is not only finding a job suiting their needs but, once they have found one, assessing if they are likely to find a better one and deciding whether it is convenient to accept the position and drop their search or continue to look for a better one remaining out of work for the time being. The cost involved in this choice, i.e. the cost of searching a job, is mainly represented by the need to remain out of work and to go on searching for a position, and is thus equal to the wages the representative worker fails to earn by giving up a job and continuing his/her search. To this we must add the outlays and stress involved in the search itself and, in general, the material and psychological disadvantages of being unemployed and in search of a job.

One of the differences between this and traditional neoclassical theory is that while in the latter a fall in wages necessarily and promptly pushes up demand for labour, according to the job search theory any such fall meets opposition from workers before it can display its effects. And this opposition is due to lack of information. To understand this, let us consider that according to this theory an economic crisis which makes it impossible to keep employment levels unaltered at the previous wage rates does not usually result in the relevant workers being fired. It causes wage reductions and, consequently, a *voluntary* exodus of those workers who are not willing to accept a reduction in their wages and start searching for jobs in which they would continue to earn their previous wage rates. Only after much searching, when these workers realize that (in the situation of crisis they gradually become aware of) they cannot find jobs at the wages they were paid before, the relevant wage reduction will produce a rise in employment because workers, having acquired additional information, will put up with lower wages.

Another highly important and innovative aspect of *job search* models is the attention they give to flows into and out of employment. In point of fact these theoretical models have been constructed to account for the fact that individuals do switch over from employment to unemployment and vice versa, for the average length of unemployment periods, etc., and for a series of different variables which, being of a temporal order, were usually neglected in classical investigations into the employment issue.[2]

3.4   NEW MICROECONOMICS. THE THEORY OF LABOUR AND THE *OPTIMAL STOPPING RULE*

The developments in neoclassical theory we are discussing here are largely based on the so-called 'new microeconomics of the labour market' of which the job search theory is a major part.

The overall picture of the job search theory provided in the previous sections can be completed by reference to numerous papers that have appeared on this subject since the 1970s. As mentioned before, this theory focuses mainly on the lack of information available and is usually based on Phelps' parable of the islands.

A basic assumption of the new microeconomics of the labour market is that workers and jobs have distinctive characteristics of their own, which is tantamount to saying that each worker is different from all the others and each job is different from all the others. In Holt's words (1970, p. 54):

> The general approach considers the worker, both in his skills and preferences, to be complex and unique. Jobs similarly are considered to have unique and complex sets of requirements and rewards.

Obviously this means that each particular firm/worker agreement will depend on a large number of circumstances of concern to one or the other party. Furthermore, the idea that workers and jobs are highly heterogeneous and that the latter may require a noticeable degree of professional specialization means that 'knowledge will be costly and highly imperfect, so that blind random search necessarily will play an important role' (Holt, 1970, p. 55).

By definition, vacancies equal the difference between demand for labour and the number of jobs filled and are created every time a job is vacated for whatever reason (dismissal or voluntary resignation) or when demand for labour increases; by the same token, the number of those unemployed is matched exactly by the supply of labour plus jobs filled; there is a continuous flow into and out of employment and those either dismissed or resigning of their own choice go to increase the numbers of those who would like to enter the labour market for the first time but are slow to find suitable jobs.

In each single period workers aspire to a given wage level which they are not prepared to renounce, the so-called 'reservation wage'; those out of work will thus continue searching for a job until they are offered a pay which is at least equal to their 'reservation wage'. According to job search theory this reservation wage decreases throughout the search. Initially it is assumed to be very high, equal to or even higher than the wage the workers concerned used to earn before (provided they had been employed previously), because whoever leaves a position in order to find another is obviously determined to improve his/her condition; yet also those who have been fired will accept lower wages only when, after much job searching, they realize that they are unable to find a job at their previous wage level. As time passes by, therefore, the workers concerned gather more and more information and, being unable to find a job, they reach the conclusion that the average wage level has decreased compared to their expectations; also, job searchers usually start considering offers which they assume to be the best and only when the earlier phase of their search has proved unsuccessful do they resolve to contact firms which are likely to offer lower pay levels; lastly, it should be noted that the costs involved in this search, especially psychological ones, increase as the job search progresses and that this, too, helps lower the reservation wage level. In Figure 3.1 the decreasing relationship between the 'reservation wage' and the time spent searching for a job is reflected by curve $\left(W_{di}\right)$, which starts out from a point (P) that marks the moment in time (t_i) when the job search begins. The wage level the worker is trying to obtain is more than W_i, which we assume was the pay the worker used to earn in his/her previous job.

Using symbols this is expressed by:

$$W_{di} = f(Tu) \qquad con \ f' < 0 \qquad (3.1)$$

where W_{di} is the wage level worker i would like to earn, i.e. his/her *reservation wage*, and Tu is the period of time during which he/she was out of work.

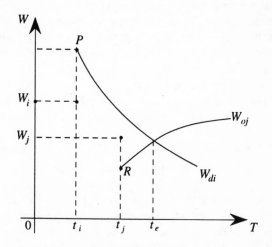

Figure 3.1   The optimal stopping rule

As is well known, the traditional static analysis of labour supply holds that a given quantity of jobs are offered for each single wage level, but that:

Although appropriate for some problems, it hardly seems the suitable tool for analyzing the short term behaviour of an unemployed worker who is head of a household. He does not have a *rigid* supply curve that governs whether or not he will accept a job offer. Rather movements of the worker's supply curve occur with the passage of time unemployed and we need a theory for predicting how these movements will occur (Holt, 1970, p. 61).

Similarly, a firm wanting to find workers with the best qualifications available in the labour market and to take them on at the lowest wage rates prevailing in that market will initially offer very low wage levels; with the passing of time, however, it will be induced to offer higher wages if it fails to find workers with appropriate qualifications. The money wage offered by a firm, j, termed W_{oj}, is consequently an increasing function of the number of vacancies available and can be written as follows:

$$W_{oj} = g(Tv) \qquad\qquad \text{con } g' > 0 \qquad (3.2)$$

where Tv is the period of time the relevant position remained unfilled. Graphically, the increasing relation between W_{oj} and the period of time Tv is reflected by the curve W_{oj}, which starts from a point, R, which identifies time t_j, i.e. the moment when the job search begins, and a wage offered lower than W_j, which we assume is the wage rate the firm used to pay in respect of that position when it was not yet vacant.

In such a situation the vacant position available will only be filled if the worker i and the firm j either meet at time t_e – the point at which the two curves meet – or even later on. After t_e an agreement is still possible because the wage the firm is willing to pay is higher than the minimum wage the worker had resolved to accept.

From the perspective of the job search theory the so-called *optimal stopping rule* can thus be formulated as follows:

– *each wage offer, W_t, will only be accepted by a worker provided it is equal to or higher than his/her reservation wage.*

Naturally, the shorter the unemployment period, Tu, the greater the number of workers who will start searching for new jobs and the shorter the time the relevant positions remain vacant, Tv, the greater the number of dismissals on the part of firms. However, it is no less true that the average length of the unemployment period is proportional to the unemployment level as a whole, because the longer people are out of job, the more difficult it becomes to find a job, *ceteris paribus*; and the greater the number of vacancies the longer the average vacancy period of a position.[3]

3.5   HOLT'S MODEL

The question now is: in what way can the considerations developed above be viewed as a different interpretation of the Phillips curve? To answer this, it will be convenient to discuss Holt's model in detail because in his attempt to explain the inverse relationship between wage increases and unemployment Holt makes explicit reference to the job search theory (see Holt, 1970).

Holt sets out from the observation that in the United Stated changes in unemployment levels over the years are very small as compared to unemployment inflows (due to dismissals, voluntary resignation or other reasons) and outflows (due to fresh hirings or other reasons). This, he argues, must mean that flows into and out of unemployment roughly cancel each other out, since otherwise, if substantial flows into unemployment were not counterbalanced by roughly equal outflows, the number of those out of work would change appreciably. 'This near equality of the gross inflow and outflow' – he writes – 'is the basis for considering the system always to be close to stochastic equilibrium' (see Holt, 1970, p. 58).

To illustrate the important aspect of how the labour market works he examines the repercussions of a sudden rise in output – an event which is known to push up demand for labour and thus to increase the number of fresh vacancies. It goes without saying that more vacancies will facilitate the search for a job and will thus result in more workers being hired and fewer being out of work, besides reducing the average unemployment period Tu and lengthening the average vacancy period Tv. These changes, which make it easier for workers to find jobs, will induce many of them to resign their positions and begin searching for better jobs, and this will in turn increase vacancies and the number of jobless. As a result, there is a greater likelihood that job seekers and employers in search of workers will actually converge and unemployment will decline to an extent which will probably counterbalance the previous rise in unemployment. In addition to this we must bear in mind that increases in demand for labour, average vacancy periods and voluntary resignations will induce firms to dismiss a smaller number of workers – a fact which in turn boosts the total number of those in employment while reducing the total number of jobless. By shortening the average unemployment period, the latter changes in turn generate a greater number of voluntary resignations, so that the resulting unemployment inflow will offset the drop in the number of jobless at least in part.

From the above it follows that the variables usually considered when analysing the labour market are interconnected in many ways and that the system is characterized by strong feedbacks, since any increase in one stock reduces the flows responsible for its increase and the stock consequently tends to return to its initial value.

At this point we will discuss three types of wage changes: changes registered when workers resign, begin their job search and manage to find fresh positions; changes observed when workers switch over from one job to another without being out of work in the interval; and changes occurring within one and the same workplace.

1. The first case reflects the typical job search theory scenario. The worker resigns in order to seek another job; with his/her reservation wage in mind[4] he/she refuses available jobs until he/she is offered an amount exceeding such reservation wage. As mentioned before, however, this amount not only declines with the passing of time, but also depends on the wage he/she used to earn previously. Thus it is reasonable to assume that at the beginning of his/her search his/her reservation wage was slightly higher than the last wage he/she earned, i.e. that:

$$W_t^{\circ}(i) = A_i W_t(i) \qquad\qquad A_i \geq 1 \qquad\qquad (3.3)$$

where $W^{\circ}(i)$ is the reservation wage of the worker i, t the time when he/she begins his search, $W_t(i)$ his/her last wage level (the worker is assumed to begin his/her search immediately upon leaving his previous job at time t, and A_i is the figure, usually greater than one, reflecting the amount by which the worker's reservation wage initially exceeds $W_t(i)$.

In Holt's model it is also assumed that the general wage level varies at a constant rate throughout the job search period and that the reservation wage is gradually adjusted in line with changes in the general wage level.

Based on the above assumptions, after the period of search Tu (which is equal to the unemployment period), the reservation wage is:

$$W_{t+Tu}^{\circ}(i) = A_i W_t(i) e^{(\dot{w}-Di)Tu} \qquad\qquad (3.4)$$

where $\dot{w}$ is the rate of variation in the general wage level and Di is the rate at which the worker's expectations diminish due to his/her unsuccessful search and the fact that he/she is still out of work.

If the search ends at time $t + Tu$, the wage rate the worker is granted upon accepting a new job must at least be equal to his/her reservation wage, so that:

$$W_{t+Tu}(i) = B_i W_{t+Tu}^{\circ}(i) \qquad\qquad B_i \geq 1 \qquad\qquad (3.5)$$

where B_i is a causal variable, equal to or greater than one, which indicates that the wage rate earned must at least equal the reservation wage, but will usually be greater.

Substituting (3.4) into (3.5), we have:

$$\frac{W_{t+Tu}(i)}{W_t(i)} = A_i B_i e^{(\dot{w}-Di)Tu} \tag{3.6}$$

Now, if $\dot{w}(i)$ is the rate of change of the wage earned by the worker i, we can write:

$$W_{t+Tu}(i) = W_t(i)e^{\dot{w}(i)Tu} \tag{3.7}$$

and, therefore, for (3.6):

$$e^{\dot{w}(i)Tu} = A_i B_i e^{(\dot{w}-Di)Tu} \tag{3.8}$$

Using logarithms, we have:

$$\dot{w}(i) = \dot{w} - Di + \frac{\lg A_i B_i}{Tu} \tag{3.9}$$

Thus the aggregate rate of change in the wages of all those who switch over to better jobs is:

$$\dot{w}_u = \dot{w} - D + \frac{\lg AB}{Tu} \tag{3.10}$$

where D, A, B and Tu are mean values for all the workers who start their search upon leaving their jobs.

The result obtained shows that the rate of growth of the wages earned by workers who find new jobs after leaving their previous positions in order to switch over to better positions equals the difference between the general rate of change in wages $\dot{w}$ and the rate at which reservation wages are seen to decline, on average, with the lengthening of the unemployment period, plus a parameter which measures the effort expended in order to obtain a wage increase, equal to $\lg AB$ divided by the average unemployment period.

The average unemployment period (expressed in months) is, by definition, equal to the unemployment stock U divided by the unemployment outflow in each period (i.e. in each month), that is:

$$Tu = \frac{U}{F} \tag{3.11}$$

where F is the unemployment outflow. Substituting (3.11) into (3.10), the result is thus:

$$\dot{w}_u = \dot{w} - D + \lg AB \, \frac{F}{U} \tag{3.12}$$

from which we can easily derive an inverse relationship between u and $\dot{w}$.

2. At this point let us consider the changes in the wage levels of those who conduct their search *on the job*, i.e. without leaving their previous workplace. Let Tc be the average period of time between each passage from one job to another. Holt makes the strange assumption that wage increases obtained when passing from one job to another are unrelated to the general wage variation rate calculated for the period Tc. Thus he holds average changes in the wages concerned to be obtained by means of the expression:

$$\frac{W_{t+Tc}}{W_t} = ABC \cdot e^{cTc} \tag{3.13}$$

where A and B reflect the values mentioned above, C is a constant, greater than 1, which reflects the greater contractual power of those employed and c is the average variation of the wages concerned.

Following similar steps to those made in the previous case, in logarithmic terms we obtain the following expression:

$$\dot{w}_c = \frac{\lg ABC}{T_c} \tag{3.14}$$

where $\dot{w}_c$ is the average variation rate in the wages of those who conduct their search on the job.

The average period of time (in months) a worker conducting his search on the job takes to switch over from one position to another is, by definition, equal to the total number of those in employment, E, divided by the number of those switching over from one position to another in each period (each month) without ever being out of work, i.e.:

$$T_c = \frac{E}{Q} \tag{3.15}$$

where Q is the flow of workers having found a better position while still in employment. Substituting (3.15) into (3.14), the result is:

$$\dot{w}_c = \lg ABC\, \frac{Q}{E} \tag{3.16}$$

3. The changes in the wage levels of those who do not change their jobs can be assumed to be equal to the average variation rate in the wages of those who conduct their search after leaving their previous positions and the variations in the wages of those who switch over to a different position without ever being out of a job; thus we obtain:

$$\dot{w}_b = k_u \dot{w}_u + k_c \dot{w}_c \tag{3.17}$$

where $\dot{w}_b$ reflects the wage variables of those who have not changed their jobs, k_u *and* k_c are *weights* and the following properties are applicable:

$$0 \le k_u \le 1 \; ; \;\; 0 \le k_c \le 1 \; ; \;\; k_u + k_c = 1$$

Equation (3.17) can be explained by observing that an employer who does not want to lose his employees will have to grant wage increases to those he wishes to keep.

Substituting (3.12) and (3.16) into (3.17), we obtain the following result:

$$\dot{w}_b = k_u \left(\dot{w} - D + \lg AB\, \frac{F}{U} \right) + k_c \, \lg ABC\, \frac{Q}{E} \tag{3.18}$$

Now that the values of $\dot{w}_u$, $\dot{w}_c$ and $\dot{w}_b$ are known, we can calculate the general rate of variation in wages as the weighted average of the changes registered in the different components, i.e.:

$$\dot{w} = u\,\dot{w}_u + (1-u)\left(\dot{w}_c + \dot{w}_b\right) \tag{3.19}$$

where the weights u and $(1 - u)$ are the percentages of workers of the different components. Substituting the values for wage changes obtained from (3.12), (3.16) and (3.18) into (3.19), we have:

$$\dot{w} = u\left(\dot{w} - D + \lg AB \frac{F}{U}\right) +$$

$$+ (1-u)\left[\lg ABC \frac{Q}{E} + k_u\left(\dot{w} - D + \lg AB \frac{F}{U}\right) + k_c \lg ABC \frac{Q}{E}\right] \quad (3.20)$$

Solving for $\dot{w}$, the result is:[5]

$$\dot{w} = -D\frac{1}{1-k_u}\left(\frac{u}{1-u} + k_u\right) +$$

$$+ \lg AB \frac{F}{U} \cdot \frac{1}{1-k_u}\left(\frac{u}{1-u} + k_u\right) + \frac{1+k_c}{1-k_u} \lg ABC \frac{Q}{E} \quad (3.21)$$

and, therefore, reorganizing:

$$\dot{w} = \frac{1}{1-k_u}\left[\left(\frac{u}{1-u} + k_u\right)\left(\lg AB \frac{F}{U} - D\right) + (1+k_c)\lg ABC \frac{Q}{E}\right] \quad (3.22)$$

In Holt's opinion the Phillips curve can be obtained by assuming that:

a. the percentage of those switching over to a different job while still in employment changes depending on the vacancies, V, which in turn change inversely to the unemployment level, U; thus we can write:

$$\frac{Q}{E} = h \cdot \frac{1}{U}$$

where h is a constant;

b. the value of $u/(1 - u)$ is small as compared to k_u;

c. the value of F is approximately constant, since in conditions of stochastic equilibrium (which, as mentioned at the beginning of this section, are the conditions assumed by Holt) the flow into unemployment is exactly matched by the relevant outflow and the two main subflows which make up the total, i.e. dismissals and voluntary resignations, vary inversely to aggregate demand and tend to cancel each other out. At this point the expression (3.21) can be written as follows:

$$\dot{w} = -D\frac{1}{1-k_u}\left(\frac{u}{1-u}+k_u\right)+$$

$$+\left[\lg AB\,(F)\frac{1}{1-k_u}\left(\frac{u}{1-u}+k_u\right)+\frac{1+k_c}{1-k_u}\lg ABC\,(h)\right]\frac{1}{U} \qquad (3.23)$$

As the value of $u/1-u$ is small as compared to k_u, the expressions between brackets in (3.23) are approximately constant. Therefore it is possible to write, with close approximation:

$$\dot{w} = a+b\frac{1}{U} \qquad (3.24)$$

which is in fact a possible way of writing a Phillips curve.

3.6 JOB SEARCH AND THE PHILLIPS CURVE IN PHELPS' INTERPRETATION

As mentioned before, an expectation-augmented Phillips curve can be constructed by recourse to the job search theory and was actually constructed by Phelps, Holt and Mortensen in 1970. Their excellent essays were simultaneously published in the (collectaneous) volume entitled *Microeconomic Foundations of Employment and Inflation* (see Phelps, 1970b) and today they are highly rated.

Phelps' contribution deals with the dynamics of wages and the hiring of workers in firms which have available incomplete information. Each firm is viewed as a sort of monopsony which will find it all the easier to hire fresh workers the more its wage levels increase as compared to the increases registered elsewhere; the wages each firm is willing to pay are assumed to become higher (as compared to those it expects other firms to pay) as the expected unemployment rate decreases and the more vacancies it thinks it has to fill. Consequently, in a situation of generalized excess demand with low unemployment and many vacancies, all the firms will be prepared to pay higher wages than those they assume are paid elsewhere.

Against the expectations of all firms, the result will be a generalized wage increase (since no firm will be able to hire fresh workers unless it pays higher wages than those paid elsewhere).

However, the decision of firms to hire more workers is not the only effect of an increase in aggregate demand. According to the job search theory, a rise in demand for labour produces a surge in the number of vacancies and this, while facilitating the search for jobs on the part of workers, makes it more difficult for the single firm to find the workers it needs; as a result, workers are encouraged to ask for even higher wages and firms to offer them. A rise in demand for labour also results in more hirings and shorter average search periods, but in periods of rising demand for labour jobs will remain vacant for a longer time (because of the increase in the number of vacancies to be filled). The effect of this is that more workers will set out to search for a job, with consequential increases in the number of jobless and vacancies and, lastly, a fall in the number of firings by firms.

Although the situation described above is one where different forces are seen to work in opposite directions, as mentioned before, it is likely that the new hirings will reduce unemployment by a rate higher than the increase in unemployment caused by workers resigning their positions voluntarily. As a rule, it follows that the rise in aggregate demand for commodities and the surge in demand for labour that this produces will push up wage levels and reduce unemployment, in line with the result of the Phillips curve (see Phelps, 1970a, 1970c; and, for a brief résumé, Phelps, 1969, pp. 152–3).

However, this Phillips curve is only valid in the short run. As the long-run Phillips curve is a vertical line even according to this interpretation, monetary or tax policies will push up real income levels only if people are 'deceived' by them to the point of mistaking nominal changes for real changes (see Maddock and Carter, 1982, p. 43); but in the long run this wrong data will be corrected and nominal changes will no longer be mistaken for real ones.

The neoclassical assumption that higher employment levels can only be created 'by surprise', i.e. through deceit, poses a problem in terms of the optimal use of resources available. In the opinion of Friedman, 'there is a tendency to take it for granted that a high level of recorded unemployment is evidence of inefficient use of resources and conversely. This view is seriously in error. A low level of unemployment may be a sign of a forced draft economy that is using its resources inefficiently and is inducing its workers to sacrifice leisure for goods that they value less highly than the leisure under the mistaken belief that their real wages will be higher than they prove to be' (Friedman, 1977; now in Friedman, 1991, p. 95).

3.7   FURTHER OBSERVATIONS ON THE JOB SEARCH THEORY AND THE PHILLIPS CURVE

The merits of Phelps', Holt's and Mortensen's contributions are still recognized today despite the negligible role the job search theory played in later approaches to the unemployment issue at least in Europe. To a large extent this depends on the fact that its basic assumption, namely high labour mobility, is only observed in the United States and is far from a realistic assumption for European labour markets; but it may also be due to the fact that no interesting contributions appeared after the initial ones mentioned before.[6]

Later studies investigated the reservation wage and the reasons why it tends to decline as the job search progresses. According to Telser, those conducting their search without having a clear picture of the prices quoted by different sellers use this time to gather information on the possible frequency distribution of prices. As the refusal of a number of jobs by a worker and the decision to continue the search are a sign that the worker concerned was offered wage levels which fell short of his/her expectations, the worker must be assumed to lower his/her expectations as the search progresses. In his contribution, Telser suggests splitting the search procedure into two successive steps: collecting information and deciding whether to make a purchase or sale. But as in the labour market it would not be realistic to assume that an offer that has once been rejected can be accepted at a later stage, these two steps are found to overlap and we can safely argue that a worker who has refused the first jobs he/she has been offered will reduce his/her acceptance wage on learning that the conditions prevailing in the market are less advantageous than he/she had originally assumed (see Telser, 1973).

Adopting a different approach to the decline in the reservation wage, Salop argues that the usual assumption that workers do not know which firms have vacancies or offer the best terms is far from realistic. In his opinion a better assumption would be that workers do not make random choices, but start by contacting the firms which they think are the best. Provided their information is not entirely wrong, this clearly implies that they are also aware that the difficulty to find higher wage positions will increase as their search progresses. And it is this that induces them to reduce their reservation wage (see Salop, 1973).

Subsequent studies on the reservation wage found that firms interview on average eight candidates before hiring one worker. Examining current interview procedures, they reached the conclusion that it is firms that usually discard candidates for their vacancies and that the reservation wage has little, if any influence on the acceptance of contracts of employment (see Barron, Bisho and Dunkelberg, 1985).

One of the assumptions of the job search theory that has often been severely criticized (see Pissarides, 1986) is the idea that the greater part of the newly unemployed are those who have left their jobs of their own choice. Showing that flows into and out of unemployment were comparatively slight in European countries and Japan for a long period following World War II, Bean, too (1992a and 1992b) brought evidence in support of the hypothesis that variations in unemployment levels do not stem from the scenario of job search theory (see, also, Smith, 1994).

Concluding, we may try to weigh up the merits of job search theory as an interpretation of the Phillips curve. One of the most convinced advocates of this possibility found that it provided a fairly good explanation of the relationship between unemployment and inflation monitored in eighteen countries between 1951 and 1967 (see Lucas, 1973, p. 334). In spite of this, it is fair to say that the assumptions behind this theory are barely applicable to the situations actually observed in most industrial countries. In Italy, for example, the industrial sector usually hires workers through the labour exchange and can only take on those unemployed, but in sectors where workers are freely hired it is those already in employment that will find new jobs more easily than the jobless (for a similar finding concerning the UK, see Sinclair, 1987; for the Italian case, see Casavola and Sestito, 1995). According to Blinder, an assumption of the job search theory is that 'search is so much more efficient off the job than on the job that the efficiency gains from searching while unemployment lasts outweigh the lost income' (i.e. the wages not earned by refusing the first job offered in order to search for a better one), but this argument is not supported by any empirical evidence and 'we know that people can search better on the job in some labour markets' (Blinder, 1988, p. 144). Data evidence shows that job seekers only devote a few hours a week to their search and seldom refuse an offer (see Clark and Summers, 1979) and it is difficult to believe that 'a few hours of search activity per week interfere unduly with holding a job' (Blinder, 1988, p. 144) unless we argue (as some indeed do) that there is a tacit agreement between employers not to steal each other's workers or that a worker conducting his search on the job is badly looked upon by possible employers because his search is evidence of scant loyalty or commitment to his current employer. In Tobin's opinion statistical evidence even suggests that most of the search for a new or better job by adults is conducted on the job (see Tobin, 1977).[7]

Lastly, the tendency of job search theory to consider all unemployment voluntary seems unrealistic even when it is applied to the United States. There, most workers leave their jobs, not of their own choice, but because they have been dismissed. Studies such as Hall's (1980) leave little room for doubt on the nature of existing unemployment, since it is anything but difficult to distinguish between workers dismissed against their will and those leaving their jobs voluntarily.

Let us emphasize again, at this point, that what makes this theory appear highly unrealistic, at least when applied to most European countries, is the scant mobility of labour. Given the high unemployment levels generally registered in recent years, those in employment hardly ever give up their jobs to search for a better one. To this we may add that while it is difficult to assume that the high levels of unemployment registered in Europe since World War II were of the frictional or voluntary type, there is no denying that the relevant unemployment was at least in part involuntary, i.e. 'Keynesian' or 'structural' (see, for instance, CEPR, 1995).[8]

3.8   CLOSING REMARKS

The conclusion which emerges from the foregoing is that while offering sound microfoundations for a neoclassical interpretation of the Phillips curve the job search theory is unable to explain unemployment for two main reasons.

First and foremost its focus is entirely on the microeconomics of labour supply. And although this doubtlessly provides a clearer picture of the mechanisms which govern the behaviour of the jobless (and those employed) when they weigh up in their minds whether they should keep a job or give it up to accept a position they have already been offered (or seek better opportunities),[9] it is clear that a theory of unemployment which claims to be complete cannot ignore the behaviour of firms or the macroeconomic aspects of the dynamics of labour supply. In this connection it will be worth noting that now that the 1990s are drawing to a close mainstream opinion tends to hold the view that 'institutions shape microeconomic behaviour' and that microeconomics should consequently have 'macroinstitutional foundations' (Fitoussi, 1995, p. xxi).

Secondly, we have already laid stress on the fact that some of the starting assumptions of the job search theory are so thoroughly in contrast with reality that it is difficult to generalize its findings.

With respect to the Phillips curve, the above reflections prompt the conclusion that although the job search theory suggests a consistent way of reconciling the neoclassical theory of the labour market with empirical findings on the unemployment–inflation trade off, it cannot be considered a convincing interpretation of this famous curve.

NOTES

1. According to some, the 'island' hypothesis 'seems to suit a society in which the fastest means of communication is the floating coconut' and not one relying on radio and television (see Maddock and Carter, 1982, pp. 44–5).
2. It is also thanks to this research direction that fresh attention was given in the 1970s to flows of population into and out of different *conditions*, thus providing further knowledge on how the labour market works. On this point, see, for example, Mortensen, 1986 and Smith, 1994, pp. 146–64.
3. For a theoretical discussion and a detailed, more thorough survey of this approach, see Mortensen, 1986.
4. Some authors prefer the phrase 'asking wage' to indicate that it is the wage demanded by workers and not that offered by firms (see Borjas, 1996, pp. 447–51).
5. According to Phelps, in Holt's model 'the general rate of increase in wages is a weighted average of the rate at which unemployed persons reduce their acceptance wage (as they learn about the wage distribution they are sampling from) and the rate at which employed persons improve their wage rates by moving from low-wage to high-wage jobs' (see Phelps, 1969, p. 152).
6. However, for the integration of the job search theory into a more general model, see Layard, Nickell and Jackman, 1991, pp. 34–40.
7. The same opinion is expressed, among others, by Isaac, 1993, p. 457.
8. For a different criticism of Alchian and Phelps' theory, see, for example, Tarantelli, 1974, pp. 26–7.
9. See Smith, 1994, pp.154–58, Pissarides, 1990, p. 69. Also Layard, Nickell and Jackman, 1991, pp. 216–7, pointing out that the job search theory makes it possible to answer questions concerning the behaviour of those unemployed, clarifies the fact that it is a 'contribution to understanding both the level of unemployment and the causes of its persistence in the aftermath of shocks.'

4   The Phillips curve and stagflation

4.1   INTRODUCTION

Many of the theoretical and empirical studies of the Phillips curve that appeared throughout the 1970s and 1980s had been conducted from a decidedly non-classical perspective and were aimed to reconcile the findings of previous analyses and interpretations with stagflation – a phenomenon in many respects incompatible with a traditional approach to the famous curve. The simultaneous presence of inflation and economic stagnation seemed indeed to contradict both Phillips' inverse relationship and one of the mainstays of macroeconomic and economic policy studies in previous decades, namely the idea of inflation and unemployment as two opposite evils. And this is the main reason why non-neoclassical theoretical constructions and empirical surveys suggested rational explanations of stagflation which can be read as criticisms of the original curve alternative to monetarists'.

In terms of economic policy, one implication of these new theories was a fresh approach to incomes policies, which were used to reverse the upward movement of the Phillips curve caused by the new variables that had been introduced into their models in order to explain its rightward movement.

With specific focus on the relations between different income policies and the Phillips curve, in this chapter we intend to discuss a few approaches which explain stagflation in the light of a 'conflict-augmented' Phillips curve (Sections 4.2–4.3) as well as a number of implications for income policy (Sections 4.4–4.6). The conclusions are preceded by a brief exposition of a different Keynesian approach to the Phillips curve (Section 4.7).

4.2   GRUBB, JACKMAN AND LAYARD'S APPROACH TO STAGFLATION: THE *CONFLICT-AUGMENTED* PHILLIPS CURVE

One explanation of stagflation which was favourably received in the 1970s and 1980s and has continued to gain credit to this day is owed to Grubb,

Jackman and Layard (see, for example, Clark and Laxaton, 1997), who developed and enhanced the Phillips curve by adding 'conflictual' elements. These authors were the first to argue that trade union pressure for higher wages is not only aimed to recover the loss in purchasing power caused by inflation, but also to pass previous increases in average labour productivity on to workers (see Grubb, Jackman and Layard, 1982).

Let the rate of growth in money wages be:

$$\dot{w}_t = \dot{p}_t^e - g\left(u_t - u_n\right) + \dot{\pi}* \qquad (4.1)$$

where $\dot{w}$ is the rate of growth in money wages, $\dot{p}_t^e$ the anticipated rate of inflation, u_n the natural rate of unemployment, u_t the actual rate of unemployment and $\dot{\pi}*$ the rate of increase in labour productivity in the last few years. Equation (4.1) is an expectation-augmented Phillips curve whose constant g reflects the rate by which a wage hike slows down when the real unemployment rate (i.e. the difference between u and u_n) increases,[1] but which is made more complex by the introduction of the term $\dot{\pi}*$. The latter is the rate of growth in labour productivity in past years, but is also assumed to reflect the *asked increase* in the real wage when equals u_n (the unemployment rate is the NRU).

More precisely, the above equation is based on the assumption that unions bargain for *real* (not money) wages and that besides pressing for money wage increases sufficient to recover the loss in the purchasing power of money expected to be caused by inflation they also demand real wage increases equal to productivity gains monitored in the last few years. Consequently $\dot{\pi}*$ reflects, at the same time, the growth in the productivity of labour actually monitored in previous years and real wage increases demanded for the near future. This hypothesis seems to be realistic enough when it is applied to an economy with comparatively low unemployment levels. In point of fact, as unions acquired greater power in factories and firms, they began to press for real wage increases commensurate with the rise in labour productivity. The idea of linking asked wage increases to actual productivity gains instead of expected ones is justified both because the former are certain (and thus a better basis for bargaining than expectations) and because workers who have once managed to push through a real pay rise equal to past productivity gains are not easily persuaded to accept lower pay rises during periods of crisis.[2] As a result of all this, it takes a few years before the wage rate can be adjusted to the changing requirements of the economy[3].

An interesting assumption behind this model is that real wages – or, rather, their (anticipated or demanded) rate of increase – are rigid downwards. As traditional Keynesian theory assumes that the *money* wage is not continuously negotiated or renegotiated, but given and constant throughout the period considered, so the modern approach we are discussing assumes the asked *real* wage (or even its rate of increase) to be fairly rigid and to generate inflation because of its slow adjustment to changes in labour productivity.[4]

Let the rate of increase in prices be:

$$\dot{p}_t = \dot{w}_t - \dot{\pi}_t \tag{4.2}$$

where $\dot{\pi}_t$ is the actual rise in productivity for the current year.

Substituting (4.1) into (4.2), we have:

$$\dot{p}_t = \dot{p}_t^e - g\left(u_t - u_n\right) + \left(\dot{\pi}^* - \dot{\pi}_t\right) \tag{4.3}$$

From (4.3) it follows that inflation rises not only when levels of activity are too high, but also when a labour productivity growth slows down and $\dot{\pi}_t$ drops to a value short of the productivity gains registered in the previous years (i.e. less than $\dot{\pi}^*$).[5]

Thus any slowdown in productivity growth rates generates inflation because unions are slow to adjust their claims to a decreasing trend in productivity; instead of putting up with lower wage increases they continue to demand the same real wage increases they used to be granted in the past. In this way they drive up labour costs and the relevant surge is promptly transferred onto prices. The most interesting point to note is that in this approach to the Phillips curve inflation is presented as the effect of slower growth, i.e. crisis; and can thus explain stagflation. In point of fact it is all but difficult to show that both prices and unemployment rise when the rate of growth in productivity declines.

Another interesting implication can be drawn from the above. Let us write (4.3) as follows:

$$\dot{p}_t = \dot{p}_t^e - g\left[u_t - \left(u_n + \frac{\dot{\pi}^* - \dot{\pi}_t}{g}\right)\right] \tag{4.4}$$

(where the last term of (4.3) has been multiplied and, at the same time, divided by g). Equation (4.4) shows that when predictions prove to be correct (i.e. if real prices actually reach the expected level), inflation slows down or accelerates depending on the following condition:

$$u_t \gtreqless u_n + \frac{\dot{\pi}^* - \dot{\pi}_t}{g}$$

The equation also confirms the assumption that the equilibrium rate of unemployment – which here is clearly a NAIRU (*Non Accelerating Inflation Rate of Unemployment*) – is also influenced by the trend in productivity gains. In point of fact the rate of unemployment at which inflation does not accelerate is:

$$\text{NAIRU} = u_n + \frac{\dot{\pi}^* - \dot{\pi}_t}{g} \qquad (4.5)$$

It is equal to u_n only if the growth rate in productivity remains constant over the years, but tends to increase when $\dot{\pi}_t < \dot{\pi}^*$ and vice versa.

Accurate empirical surveys conducted by several authors in the 1980s have shown that this model can satisfactorily explain the stagflationary trend which was observed in nineteen advanced capitalist countries in the 1970s.[6] These authors argued that for one reason or another *per capita* output in industrial countries increased less in the 1970s than in previous years; but as people had got accustomed to the higher incomes afforded by soaring output levels in the 1950s and 1960s, in the 1970s pressure for more pay proved stronger than those countries could afford and ended up by triggering an inflationary surge.[7]

The above is in keeping with the so-called 'real-wage resistance approach', a theory of inflation which is still valid world-wide today and is at times *contrasted* with theories based on the Phillips curve. The rationale behind it is that union pressure aims to oppose real wage reductions and keep the real wage level stable. This is why the theorists of this approach introduce a term for the real wage levels of prior periods into their wage determination equations. Union bargaining is viewed as a process in which asked money wage increases either reflect the unions' attempt to defend the real wage level prevailing at the time or, more generally, their endeavour to continue securing, in periods with lower growth rates, those same real wage percentage increases which they deem possible in the light of their recent experience. Although this approach takes no account of expected inflation, in practice it triggers a self-fertilizing price hike process since the attempts of workers to defend the purchasing power of their real wages will inevitably push up money wages.[8]

4.3   SLOW GROWTH, CONFLICT AND INFLATION

One variant of the slow-growth-inflation model explains increases in asked real wages by reference not only to past labour productivity gains, but also to the extent of social conflict observed in the country concerned. According to this variant, wage claims are slow to adapt to varying rises in labour productivity and this adjustment will even be slower in countries where social – or, better still, industrial – relations are less consensus-based.

One possible explanation of the rigidity, or slow pace of adjustment, of real wages from the perspective of the existing degree of social consensus is linked to the general problem of the amount of information on current trends workers have access to and reflects arguments that were first propounded by Alchian and Demsetz in a well-known paper (see Alchiann and Demsetz, 1972). The idea is that workers usually have a very vague picture of their own 'contribution' to productivity (the average and marginal productivity of their work) and, through sheer lack of trust, are not willing to rely on the data provided to them on the subject by employers and/or the government. Accordingly, the more workers trust their employers, i.e. the better the 'industrial relations' or the lower the tensions between opposing factions, the more readily will workers believe the past labour productivity figures disclosed by employers and governments and the predictions based on such data, and all the more rapidly will real wage levels be brought into line with labour productivity. According to an interpretation by Hicks which goes back to 1963, most strikes are caused by uncertainties or imperfect information on the real situation of firms, so that a satisfactory degree of worker/employer trust will tend to reduce employer/worker conflicts and the number of strikes by easing negotiations and exchanges of information (see Hicks, 1963, pp. 140–52). According to other economists, however, the link between real wage rigidity and social conflict is even more direct because workers usually go on strike to defend or increase existing *real* wage levels and the number and duration of such strikes are strictly associated with existing industrial relations.

These two explanations of the link between real wage rigidity and social conflict assume that asked wage increases are associated both with the past trend in productivity and the current situation of industrial relations, e.g. they suggest a formula of the following type:

$$\dot{w}_t - \dot{p}_t^e = \alpha \left(\dot{w}_{t-1} - \dot{p}_{t-1} \right) + (1 - \alpha)\, \dot{\pi}_t \qquad (4.6)$$

where the left-hand side is the asked real wage increase rate, $\dot{w}_{t-1} - \dot{p}_{t-1}$ is the rate of increase in real wages that was achieved in the previous period,

$\dot{\pi}_t$ is the current rate of growth in labour productivity and α is a value, between zero and one, which is assumed to be the greater the more intense the social conflict is found to be. This formula shows that in periods of rising social conflict the impact of past trends on the asked real wage increase rate is greater and that of current productivity gains is smaller. Accordingly, distinguishing between two extreme cases we have:

1. with social conflict at its highest, α is equal to one, the real wage rate claimed today is only affected by wage increases obtained in the past and the real wage increase proves absolutely rigid with respect to changes in productivity:

$$\dot{w}_t - \dot{p}_t^e = \dot{w}_{t-1} - \dot{p}_{t-1}$$

2. with social conflict at its lowest, α is zero and the real wage level, being affected only by current increases in labour productivity, is highly flexible:

$$\dot{w}_t - \dot{p}_t^e = \dot{\pi}_t$$

If we now assume:

a. that the past rate of increase in real salaries was exactly matched by the average rate of growth in labour productivity, i.e.:

$$\dot{w}_{t-1} - \dot{p}_{t-1} = \dot{\pi}_{t-1} \tag{4.7}$$

b. that productivity is currently increasing at a lower rate:

$$\dot{\pi}_t < \dot{\pi}_{t-1} \tag{4.8}$$

c. that, as assumed in the previous paragraph, the actual rate of increase in prices is:

$$\dot{p}_t = \dot{w}_t - \dot{\pi}_t \tag{4.9}$$

substituting (4.6) and (4.7) into (4.9) we have:

$$\dot{p}_t = \alpha \left(\dot{\pi}_{t-1} - \dot{\pi}_t \right) + \dot{p}_t^e \tag{4.10}$$

From (4.10) it follows that the *unexpected* inflation rate is:

$$\dot{p}_t - \dot{p}_t^e = \alpha \left(\dot{\pi}_{t-1} - \dot{\pi}_t \right) > 0 \qquad (4.11)$$

based on the assumption (4.8).

Accordingly unexpected inflation depends both on the reduction in productivity gains and on the level of social conflict.

Lastly, under the fairly simpler 'adaptive' expectation hypothesis (static expectation hypothesis) according to which:

$$\dot{p}_t^e = \dot{p}_{t-1}$$

we have:

$$\dot{p}_t - \dot{p}_{t-1} = \alpha \left(\dot{\pi}_{t-1} - \dot{\pi}_t \right) \qquad (4.12)$$

From (4.12) it follows that on the assumptions previously made inflation will accelerate or decelerate as the labour productivity growth rate rises or falls, but the pace of such acceleration/deceleration will depend on the degree of social conflict currently experienced in the country concerned.

To explain stagflation it will suffice to state that any analysis intended to account for the links between slow growth, conflict and inflation from the perspective of the Phillips curve would have to combine together all the elements discussed in this and the previous sections, because in this way the co-existence of inflation and unemployment would result from the interactions between the elements considered and economic policy choices. Stagflation is indeed an unavoidable outcome if the slowdown in productivity is coupled with restrictive economic policies enforced within a conflictual context.[9]

Lastly, let us mention that a number of econometric studies conducted years ago reached the interesting conclusion that the different inflation rates monitored in OECD countries in the 1970s and 1980s could be explained by analysing the relations between conflict and the kind of inflation discussed here (see McCallum, 1983, 1986; Cornwall, 1994, mainly pp. 129–151).

4.4 THE PHILLIPS CURVE AND INCOME POLICY: A GENERAL ASSESSMENT

The augmented Phillips curves discussed in the previous sections of this chapter induced economists to rethink the implications of income policies: if the terms of the unemployment–inflation trade-off worsen as a result of social conflict and the costs of achieving price stability or full employment increase, income policies can be the right answer since they reduce pressure for wage increases at each unemployment level.[10]

As a matter of fact, a number of different meanings can be read into the phrase 'income policy'. In its original definition it describes policies aimed to slow down price increases by preventing rises in money wages, but in a wider sense it is a policy geared toward controlling all incomes – profits no less than incomes from employment – and keeping down the prices fixed by firms. Income policies are framed to fight inflation, but from a more traditional perspective wage reductions can play a role in boosting employment and in Italy, for example, income policies have even been viewed as a means of reducing consumption levels (by checking wage increases) and thus fostering investment and economic growth.[11] In other words, the term 'income policy' has been used to describe different measures intended to retard surges in money incomes. A useful distinction is that between institutional policies and *market* income policies and, among the former, between 'consensus-based' and 'coercive' policies (for a different classification, see Cornwall, 1983, pp. 248–50).

These categories of policies will be dealt with in the next section. For the time being it will be convenient to explore the extent to which the thesis that income policies shift the Phillips curve toward the origin of the axes of the graph[12] or flatten it out[13] is supported by theoretical evidence.

Among more orthodox economists there is general consensus that income policies shift the Phillips curve downward (or to the left) not because they reduce social conflict, but because they affect expectations. As mentioned above, the typical neoclassical Phillips curve is an 'expectation-augmented' curve, which means that the Phillips curve will move downward provided such income policies as have been enforced succeed in generating the belief that price increases will slow down. By its very nature, any income policy is indeed an arrangement aimed to put a check on the rates of increase in all money incomes and to slow down production costs and prices. This is why people conceive the idea that a successfully enforced income policy will slow down inflation expectations and drive the Phillips curve downward.

According to Laidler, 'the key to breaking the expectations link in the wage–price spiral involves convincing those involved in wage bargaining that past evidence on price increases is not a reliable indicator of what is going to happen in the future' (Laidler, 1971, p. 87) because the situation will take a different turn in consequence of the enforcement of a political measure – namely an income policy. Authors with a distinctively neoclassical background are sceptical about the effectiveness of such a policy. If a government announces its intention to retard inflation by enforcing appropriate income policies, they argue, this announcement will only be effective if the relevant measures are actually credible and reliable. And there is no reason to assume, they continue, that people will place greater trust on income policies than, for instance, on restrictive monetarist policies (Laidler, 1971, pp. 86–7).

A different explanation of why income policies are capable of effectively contrasting stagflationary trends and shifting the Phillips curve toward the origin was suggested in the previous sections. Actually, according to the model we discussed there, 'consensus-based' income policies can shift the Phillips curve downward and to the left by reducing social conflict.[14] The assumption behind this thesis is that in an economic system left to itself the money income determination mechanism is far from efficient and tends towards sub-optimal positions.[15] As in other cases of 'market failure', the government is simply obliged to take action if greater efficiency is to be achieved.

The issue can be discussed in the light of game theory, by looking upon the price and wage determination process as a sort of 'prisoner's dilemma' (see Maital and Benjaminini, 1980, pp. 459–81; Sutcliffe, 1982, pp. 574–85; Cornwall, 1994, pp. 92–4). In extremely simplified terms, we will assume that both capitalists and workers have a choice between two 'strategies': substantial or small income increases (which means that they can opt for high or small increases in prices and wages respectively). We will also assume that they make their decisions simultaneously and that upon choosing its strategy either class ignores the decision made (or to be made) by the other.

At this point the situation has all the characteristics of a 'non-cooperative game'. We will also make the following additional hypotheses:

a. each group will secure its maximum payoff provided it couples its own aggressive strategy with the moderate strategy of the other group; here the group that opts for a moderate strategy obtains a very low payoff;
b. inflation has an adverse impact on economic growth; when a rise in prices generates an inefficient allocation of resources, worsens the foreign constraints and triggers restrictive economic policies, the payoffs associated with the case in which both players opt for an aggressive strategy are low compared to those associated with the case in which they both choose moderate strategies.

At this point the 'game' takes on the characteristics of the 'prisoner's dilemma' and can be described using the following payoff matrix:

		WORKERS	
		A	**M**
C A P **A**		1 , 1	3 , 0
I T A L I S **M**		0 , 3	2 , 2
T S			

where *A* stands for the aggressive strategy and *M* for the moderate one, while the first figure in each quadrant stands for the payoff of capitalists and the second one for the payoff of workers.

In this case, strategy *AA*, i.e. the choice of an aggressive strategy by both classes, is the only solution associated with the payoffs 1 , 1. It corresponds to a *Nash equilibrium*[16] because it is the maxi-minimum situation in which either class has made its choice between two strategies in such a way as to avoid the risk of obtaining the lowest payoff.[17]

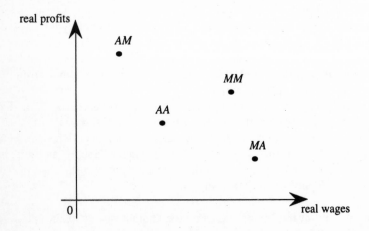

Figure 4.1   Income distribution and macroeconomic outcome

The different positions associated with the choices made by the two classes can also be graphically represented. In Figure 4.1 the axes respectively reflect real profit levels and real wage levels.

Although *MM*, the situation in which both classes choose a moderate strategy, is a Pareto-optimal,[18] it fails to achieve an equilibrium within the game because each class will find it more convenient to choose the aggressive strategy once the other has opted for moderation: thus the Nash equilibrium point *AA* is the inevitable outcome.

Considering that the graph of the game in Figure 4.1 is a – highly stylized and simplified – representation of the mechanism which generates 'conflict' inflation, we have a typical case of market failure in which the government is called upon to restore a mechanism which brings about an optimum. At this point, the question is what kind of policy can influence the result of the game.[19]

Public policy should be geared toward modifying the payoff matrix, for instance by enforcing taxes, granting tax relief or launching policies designed to discourage behaviours which trigger inflation or reward moderation, and thus toward modifying the situation and establishing a different hierarchy for the payoffs associated with different solutions of the game.

After the enforcement of a political measure such as 'a tax on the option for an aggressive strategy', the payoff matrix will change as follows:

		WORKERS	
		A	M
C A P I T A L I S T S	A	(1–2) , (1–2)	(3–2) , 0
	M	0 , (3–2)	2 , 2

At this point both classes will find it in their interests to opt for a moderate strategy because the payoff associated with this choice is in any case higher than that associated with the aggressive strategy – in respect of which the Government has enforced a disincentive.

Public policies can also take the form of tax reliefs or, more generally, 'benefits' granted to those whose behaviour does not trigger an inflationary surge. Typically, such tax reliefs could be made dependent on the choice of a moderate behaviour by the social parties,[20] so that the payoff matrices (4.13) and (4.14) will be:

		WORKERS	
		A	M
C A P I T A L I S T S	A	1 , 1	3 , (0 + 2)
	M	(0 + 2) , 3	(2 + 2) , (2 + 2)

In this case, the tax relief adds up with the payoffs associated with moderate strategies, so that the benefits associated with moderate strategies are in any case greater than the payoffs of aggressive ones.

The conclusion is that income policy, by changing the benefits associated with single strategies, may 'drive down' the Phillips curve because it removes all or part of the causes which trigger the price–wage spiral even when unemployment levels are comparatively high.

4.5   A CLASSIFICATION OF INCOME POLICIES

As mentioned before, the dynamics of wages and prices can be interfered with in a variety of ways. A thoroughly convincing classification of income policies should distinguish between institutional and market policies and, within the former category, between 'coercive' and 'consensus-based' policies.

Coercive income policies range from pay and/or price freezes to the simple enunciation of rules to govern the conduct of firms and trade unions. Wage and/or price freezes must obviously be very short-lived and are bound to come up against great difficulties. Particularly in a market economy, where firms have access to a huge spectrum of methods enabling them to side-step the relevant provisions, it needs a very efficient government structure to force through even a price freeze covering a limited category of commodities, at the other end of the spectrum the mere enunciation of 'rules' is by its very nature bound to be of little or no consequence.

A consensus-based income policy, the so-called 'social pact', can be engineered between workers, firms and the government. It can either be based on an 'economic exchange' or on a 'political exchange' between these social forces. In either case the political authorities play a substantial role in facilitating the agreement between firms and workers by granting tax relief or other benefits to the social parties that accept proposals deemed to be advantageous for the macroeconomic scenario in its entirety. When the exchange is of the 'economic' type, the government promises financial benefits in exchange for moderate wage increase pressure or the promise by employers to abstain from passing the increases in labour costs on to prices. When a 'political exchange' is opted for, the relevant agreement acquires a wider scope, since unions may prove willing to 'bargain' for lower wage increases with political measures of concern to workers (or other citizens), for instance investment in backward regions of the country, aids to developing countries, environment protection measures, etc.

Then there are the so-called 'market' income policies. The best-known among these is the TIP (Tax-Tied Income Policy), which was proposed by S. Weintraub in the early 1970s and again by Layard, Jackman and others in the 1980s (see Weintraub, 1978a, pp. 123–62; 1978b, pp. 251-321; Jackman, Layard and Pissarides, 1986 and Layard, Nickell and Jackman, 1991, pp. 485–90; Elliot, 1991, pp. 458–9). This approach involves penalizing (or rewarding) inflationary (anti-inflationary) behaviour by means of the tax lever.

Another 'market' income policy with similar theoretical foundations to those of the TIP is the MAP (*Market Anti-inflation Plan*), which was first proposed by Lerner and Colander (see Lerner and Colander, 1979, pp. 210–20) and then further discussed by several authors in recent years (see Koford and Miller, 1992; Colander, 1992; Vickrey, 1992). One way to enforce a MAP would be to make permits to adjust prices dependent on a precise production indicator. As some firms would be authorized to adjust prices more than others, a *tradable permit system* would arise in which every 'permit to trigger inflation' would be bought and purchased at a price determined by the play of demand and supply: this would internalize the *negative externalities* of inflationary price decisions made by firms and consequently reduce inflation.

Among the criticisms raised against income policies, let us mention here the general objections of monetarists who hold income policies to be at best ineffectual. According to them trade union activity affects, not inflation, but unemployment and, even more generally, they deny the very existence of cost-push inflation. In their opinion inflation is to be blamed on the monetary authorities because it is they that are responsible for excess supply of money. In periods of excess supply of money, they argue, income policies may temporarily retard wage and price increases, but in the long run they will prove ineffectual because sooner or later prices do adjust to the supply of money. Moreover, they consider income policies dangerous because they hamper the free working of market mechanisms.[21]

However, monetarist criticisms stem from their acceptance of both the quantitative theory of money and the hypothesis that the labour market can be properly described using a traditional supply and demand curve. Sharing none of these theoretical assumptions, non-neoclassical economists are inclined to consider money supply an endogenous factor and the labour market a very particular market where social and institutional factors carry great weight.

No clearcut evidence is available concerning the effectiveness of income policies. Few statistical surveys had been conducted on this topic until some years ago. However Grubb, 1986, found that a simple correlation between changes in money wages and changes in the level of demand and the general price level fails to account for about half the changes in inflation and suggested that income policies would probably provide the missing link.

In more recent studies many authors[22] tested the correlation between macroeconomic performance and the industrial relation system and obtained a hump-shaped curve: as can be seen from Figure 4.2, the best macroeconomic performance was either reached in systems with decentralized industrial relations or in systems with centralized industrial relations, while medium centralized countries presented less favourable unemployment and/or inflation figures.

According to Henley and Tsakalotos (1993, pp. 57–60), 'the hump-shaped relationship between the degree of bargaining centralization and coordination and unemployment performance' can be explained as follows. In a strongly centralized context, following a shock real wage reductions can be reached through 'consensual' agreement, while in a country with a decentralized industrial relations system they can be reached through the 'market'. In intermediate cases trade unions have at the same time the power and the duty to fight against real wage reductions because they are unable to control their effects.

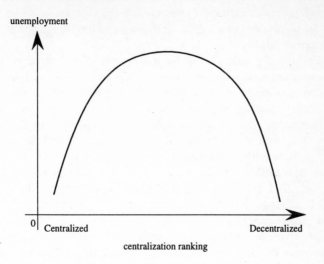

Figure 4.2   Centralization of IRS and macroeconomic performance

According to Pekkarinen, Pohjula and Rowthorn (1992, pp. 4 and 104–5), this result is the consequence of the fact that the free-riding behaviour of trade unions is only possible and convenient in the case of a medium centralized industrial system, because in such a situation trade unions are still strong enough to obtain wage increases, but lack the strength required to engineer a 'political exchange'.

4.6   THE PHILLIPS CURVE, INCOME POLICIES AND THE SYSTEM OF INDUSTRIAL RELATIONS

The literature investigating the theoretical foundations of income policies has stressed that the success or failure of economic policies enforced to slow down the growth of money incomes is mainly determined by the system of industrial relations, i.e. the bulk of rules which govern the organization of work in firms and society at large. Moreover, to a large extent the particular income policy applicable to a given economic system may depend on what 'industrial relations' prevail in the country concerned.

Though strictly interrelated, these two issues are of a quite different order and call into question the role of the Phillips curve as an analytical framework: if the success of income policies depends on the type of industrial relations, why should we continue discussing the existence of a relationship between unemployment and wage increases?

But let us proceed in a logical fashion by addressing preliminarily the first question raised.

Concerning the role played by the system of industrial relations in determining the success of an income policy, the reason why success has been held to increase in proportion to the degree of centralization is that larger trade union organizations are in a position to carry on centralized wage bargaining. The more the solution of conflict is in the hands of 'nation-wide' unions, the higher the chances for a real 'political exchange' and the more 'credible' the parties' commitment to policies of moderation (see Oswald, 1985, pp. 160–93; see, also, Flanagan, Soskice and Ulman, 1983, pp. 21–37; Henley and Tsakalotos, 1995, pp. 190–94). And a political exchange is certainly the most effective means of achieving the desired macroeconomic results.

In other words, centralization adds to the effectiveness of income policies both directly, by making central decisions more efficient, and indirectly, making expectations concerning inflation more credible. In point of fact, in a non-centralized industrial relations system union action inevitably sparks off inflationary pressures since each union will be induced, by reason of its smaller size, to breach the wage moderation 'rule' for at least two reasons:

1. a small union will assume that its conduct (pressure for substantial wage increases), being referred to a limited number of people, will have negligible macroeconomic repercussions on the general rate of inflation and will prove highly advantageous to those eligible for the wage agreements it will enter into;
2. in a multi-union scenario with numerous wage agreements the 'improper' behaviour of one free-riding union will barely be perceived by public opinion, since it is certainly more difficult to monitor the trend in wages in a situation where one has to take into account a huge body of different data than in one with few wage agreements and few nation-wide unions.

Hence the idea of the Italian economist Tarantelli to view the free-riding conduct of small unions against the background of the theory of public goods:[23] considering 'price stability' a public good whose benefits must be enjoyed by all the components of a given national community, a single small union organization will find it convenient to avoid paying the cost of this public good because this does not entail, in itself, being excluded from its benefits. It goes without saying that in the event the same conduct were adopted by all unions, no such public good as 'price stability' would be generated and the prevailing result would be an inflationary surge.[24]

Although the line of reasoning adopted above would speak for a centralized industrial relations system, this is founded on the fundamental prerequisite of the acceptance, on the part of the large union, of the principle that price stability is a 'good'. This means that the union concerned must be ideologically prepared to strike a 'political bargain' and not bent on head-on collision with the capitalist system. Only in this case will it abstain from using its power to combat the system.[25]

As for the second issue, i.e. the problem of the link between the degree of centralization of the industrial relations system and the kind of income policy to be enforced, we will confine ourselves to just a few reflections on non-centralized industrial relations systems in the light of what has been said before. First of all it is clear that the so-called 'institutional' income policies (see the definition proposed in Section 4.5) do not fit in with low union-centralization scenarios; as the relevant actions entail 'political bargaining' and will produce the desired effects only if union representatives have the power to bind local economic agents to the decisions they make, collective wage agreements entered into in situations with a low degree of union centralization would not be credible and would consequently be bound to failure.

In a non-centralized system there is more scope for the success of 'market' income policies (see definition in Section 4.5), which are not dependent on rules of conduct voluntarily subscribed to by the social parties in purposely drawn up agreements backed up by effective sanctions for those who breach the rules. They are based on indirect incentives for moderate modes of conduct and produce their effects by modifying choices made by operators; accordingly their successful implementation is not dependent on the conditions which, as mentioned before, are a prerequisite for the success of institutional income policies.

As for the Phillips curve, while the above propositions would remain irreconcilable with the finding of the original curve – a stable inflation–unemployment relationship – even if thorough social and institutional changes were enforced, they are quite evidently in line with the Phillips curve provided this is augmented by a variable reflecting political and institutional changes capable of affecting performance in individual economic contexts.

A different empirical finding was obtained following a cross-section analysis of the unemployment–inflation relationship based on average data collected in 18 OECD countries over the span of 15 years (see Cornwall, 1994, pp. 88–90; 106–8). According to this, the Phillips curve has a horizontal shape because the inflation rate is entirely independent of the unemployment rate and the different trends in unemployment levels monitored across countries can be traced back to the different political and institutional systems in force there. However, the Phillips curve we are addressing here is clearly very different from the curve which Phillips studied in 1958 and which was then re-elaborated in subsequent theoretical and empirical analyses.

4.7   A FURTHER CRITICISM OF NRU THEORY: THE DECREASING LONG-TERM PHILLIPS CURVE

A different criticism of the monetarist theory of the natural rate of unemployment was levied by those who associate the decreasing shape of the long-term Phillips curve with the fact that the parameter which links actual inflation to expected inflation is less than 1. But this subject should be addressed step by step.

Let us write the short-term Phillips curve in the following form:

$$\dot{w}_t = a - g(u_t - u_n) + c\dot{p}_t^e + \pi* \tag{4.13}$$

where the symbols have their usual meanings and a, g and c are constant. Based on equation (4.2) and with the substitutions already suggested in previous sections, we obtain the following expression:

$$\dot{p}_t = a - g(u_t - u_n) + c\dot{p}_t^e + (\pi* - \pi_t) \tag{4.14}$$

In the event of static expectations – i.e. when $\dot{p}_t^e = \dot{p}_{t-1}$ – we obtain:

$$\dot{p}_t = a - g(u_t - u_n) + c\dot{p}_{t-1} + (\pi* - \pi_t) \tag{4.15}$$

In a situation of long-term equilibrium, i.e. when $\dot{p}_t = \dot{p}^e = \dot{p}_{t-1}$, we have:

$$\dot{p}_t = \frac{a - g(u_t - u_n) + (\pi* - \pi_t)}{1 - c} \tag{4.16}$$

Equation (4.16) is a long-term Phillips curve which has a negative slope whenever the value of c is less than 1.[26] Setting out from a Keynesian interpretation of the way the labour market works, the hypothesis that $c < 1$ [27]

can be explained in a variety of different ways which, as suggested in Cornwall and Cornwall (1997, p. 528), centre on the fact that unions bargain, nor for real wages, but for money wages. As a result, the inability of unions or workers to push through wage increases in line with their expectations may be traced back to a number of reasons. On closer analysis, the awareness that money wages are the real object of union bargaining and that the real wage is determined within the commodities markets may even lead us to criticize all those who, assuming (though not providing any evidence) that bargaining concerns real wages, suggest a long term value of $c = 1$ as a corollary of the principle of rationality and conclude that the long-term Phillips curve is vertical. As Galbraith recently wrote (1997, p. 95), we should never forget that only the money wage is determined in the labour market, while the real wage is determined within the commodities market.[28]

A further implication of the fact that bargaining concerns money wages is that 'no labour supply curve exists' (see Tuchscherer, 1979, pp. 97–99 and 1984, pp. 528–30; Jossa, 1992, pp. 180–2; Galbraith, 1997, p. 95). And this is one of the reasons why a decreasing long-term Phillips curve comes to the rescue of Keynesian theory since when a Phillips relationship is assumed to be decreasing even in the long run, aggregate demand can be tackled in such a way as to permanently reduce unemployment and economic policy means re-aquire a role as macroeconomic stabilizing factors.

As will be shown in Chapter 6, these subjects have recently been addressed in theorizations concerning the hysteresis of the natural rate of unemployment and have resulted in rehabilitating the economic theories of the Keynesian school.

4.8   CONCLUSION

In this Chapter we have examined a number of non-monetarist versions of the Phillips curve which were worked out in order to account for the stagflation phenomenon. Introducing elements of 'realism' into the neoclassical theoretical framework, these new models led to a noticeable result: the point at which the Phillips curve intersects the abscissa is no longer an NRU (at which demand for labour equals supply) and thus independent of the economic policies that are framed, but a NAIRU, which is influenced by the institutions prevailing in the labour market and thus by the economic policies in place from time to time (so that the jobless may well include some who are involuntarily unemployed).

NOTES

1. More precisely, g *is* a constant which indicates the rate by which the money wage hike slows down for each one-point increase in u_r.
2. As has been observed, a slow (or only partial) adjustment of the real wage to the rates of growth in labour productivity can be a perfectly *rational* behaviour when even a union accepting the idea that unemployment increases in periods of rising real wage levels doubts that productivity may further rise in future (see Brunner, Cukierman, Meltzer, 1980); but in the next section we will show that such a behaviour is strictly associated with social conflict.
3. Obviously the rigidity of the wage structure also depends on the types of institutions prevailing in the labour markets of single countries. See Akerlof, Dickens and Perry, 1996.
4. This argument might thus be considered a more modern approach to the issue of 'relative' wages dealt with by Keynes (see Keynes, 1936, chapter II), even though attention is focused on real wages. In this connection, however, the decisive element is the institutions, for instance index-linking, etc., prevailing on the labour markets in single countries. On this point, see Destefanis, 1991.
5. In this paragraph we are focusing attention on the acceleration in the rate of growth of prices. Actually, a major part of the literature on inflation produced in the 1970s shifted attention from price increases to the acceleration in inflation rates or to unexpected inflation (these two notions coincide when $\dot{p}_t^e = \dot{p}_{t-1}$).
6. See Grubb, Jackman and Layard, 1982. See, also, for results obtained with an analogous model, Layard, Nickell and Jackman, 1991, pp. 402-36. Basing his estimates on a model used for 18 OECD countries, Cornwall, 1994, pp. 138–45. also obtained satisfactory results.
7. Among those who explained the world-wide inflationary surge in the 1970s' in this way, let us mention, for example, the Nobel-prize winner J. Meade (see Meade, 1982).
8. The real wage resistance hypothesis was developed by the Cambridge Economic Policy Group (CEPG) in the mid-seventies and was then circulated in a huge variety of models similar to the one being discussed here. See Cripps, 1977, Cripps and Godley, 1976; see also Cornwall, 1994, pp. 152–60 and 192. For an interesting re-elaboration of the real wage resistance hypothesis, see Elliot, 1991, pp. 509–11.
9. This idea was expressed, for instance, in Tarantelli, 1974 and 1986, pp. 381–6, who argued that where economic policy-makers fix a

'ceiling' for 'tolerated inflation', exogenous wage hike spirals are likely to result in a stagflationary trend. A similar thesis was set forth in Cornwall, 1994, pp. 163–5.

10. Valuable introductions to the traditional ideas on income policies are found in Jones, 1973; Fallick and Elliot, 1981 and Roncaglia, 1986.

11. See Napoleoni, 1966, which clearly discusses arguments for the thesis that workers can be expected to accept income policies only when these are coupled with investment planning.

12. See, for example, McConnel and Brue, 1995, pp. 583–4.

13. This is how the situation is presented in Cornwall, 1994, pp. 91–4.

14. This is the thesis propounded for instance in Colander, 1992, pp. 335–40. According to Layard, Nickell and Jackman (1991, pp. 485–9), a similar reduction in the NAIRU is even observed when the 'efficiency-wages' hypothesis is introduced into the model.

15. Keynes (1940, pp. 370 and 376-7) has analysed adverse macroeconomic externalities associated with the choices of businessmen and workers with respect to prices and wages (see, also, Baumol, 1952, p. 141). Concerning the impulse toward inflation inherent in price and wage determination mechanisms, see also Scitovsky, 1978, pp. 221-33.

16. A *Nash equilibrium* is registered when 'no player has incentive to deviate from his strategy given that the other players do not deviate' (Rasmusen, 1990, p. 33).

17. The game can obviously be further complicated in order to account for additional aspects of real situations and, above all, the fact that in reality the game is repeated. In this Section, however, our aim was only to show how the game theory can describe a theoretical foundation of income policy.

18. The assumption is that the macroeconomic outcome is obtained summing up the payoffs of the two players. See Maital and Benjaminini, 1980, where also different payoff matrices are discussed.

19. It has been noted that this would necessitate the introduction of a third player, namely the State with strategies, payoffs, etc. of its own (see Maddock and Carter, 1981–82, pp. 330–1). However, this problem, no less than others generated by simplified models of real scenarios, is not considered here. For a more elaborate and complete model, see Brunetta e Carraro, 1992.

20. In a similar proposal for Italy made some time ago, Sylos Labini (1985, pp. 559–74) suggested, among other possibilities, the reimbursement of the fiscal drag in subsequent years.

21. See Paish, 1971, which contains a critical discussion of British experience in matters of income policy.

22. The hump-shaped relation was first presented by Calmfors and Driffil, 1988. For a survey on this issue, see Pohjula, 1992, pp. 44–81. Many empirical results on the effects of income policies are presented in a book edited by Pekkarinen, Pohjula and Rowthorn (1992).

23. As in the example of negative external repercussions on choices concerning the determination of prices and wages, here we are again dealing with a case of 'market failure'.

24. For a different opinion on the subject, see Layard, Nickell and Jackman, 1991, p. 485. According to them centralized income policies, though enabling the economy to reach the NAIRU more rapidly and at a lower cost, can at best be assumed to be effective in the short run; according to them, only 'market' policies can produce permanent shifts in the NAIRU.

25. Tarantelli addressed this problem repeatedly in his work. In a 1981 article he wrote, for example: 'A reverse scenario is that of a system of industrial relations where a single nation-wide union organization carries on its activity within a politically and ideologically adversarial context. But this is a case in which wage and price stability is not necessarily a public good in itself' (see Tarantelli, 1981, p. 184).

26. As far as the United States is concerned, there is widespread agreement that c can be estimated at a value of near one (see, *inter alia*, Gordon, 1997, pp. 24–7). A decreasing long-term Phillips Curve might be applicable to many European countries where the values obtained from empirical estimates are much more uncertain.

27. See, *inter alia*, Tarantelli, 1986, pp. 539–49, Cornwall, 1994, pp. 152–69; Palley, 1996, pp. 166–181.

28. It has been observed that the most important implication of the NAIRU hypothesis is that most of the changes in the rate of inflation originate in the labour market and are quantitatively determined by the tensions in this market, i.e. by the unemployment rate (see Stiglitz, 1997, p. 4; for a contrasting view, see Staiger, Stock and Watson, 1997). This thesis is far from convincing since changes in the inflation rates can also be traced back to a decreasing long-term Phillips Curve, i.e. a hypothesis conflicting with the NAIRU theory. On the contrary, to trace back changes in the inflation rate to tensions within the labour market – and thus to changes in the wage level – is tantamount to conforming to Keynesian theory, which is corroborated by the assumption that real wages are determined within the commodities market.

5   Unorthodox interpretations of the Phillips curve

5.1   INTRODUCTION

Some non-neoclassical interpretations of the Phillips curve depart sharply from the traditional approach to the labour market because they address the unemployment-inflation trade-off from the perspective of a Marxist or Kaleckian approach to the social and economic issues of capitalism.

The common denominator behind them is that the impact of changes in the unemployment rate on inflation is traced back to mechanisms which differ thoroughly from those assumed in the neoclassical and Keynesian synthesis tradition discussed so far.

In this chapter we will discuss the unorthodox reconstructions of the Phillips curve proposed by Rowthorn (see Sections 5.3–5.4) and Myatt (see Sections 5.5 and 5.6). Though diverging from each other in many respects, in fact they have in common the idea that the relation between unemployment and inflation is basically determined by a conflict over income distribution.

5.2   ROWTHORN'S MODEL

In a paper published in 1977 Rowthorn proposed a precise analysis of the theoretical links that can explain the inverse relationship between unemployment and inflation, albeit along different paths from those proposed in neoclassical analyses. Recently he has reproposed this framework (Rowthorn, 1995 and 1996), which is in fact a noticeable attempt to investigate the causes of inflation and the role of money and expectations in the inflationary process in original though rigorously Marxist terms (see Rowthorn, 1977) and an explicit formulation of the Phillips curve in terms which tie in with Marx's ideas on the industrial reserve army.

To describe Rowthorn's model we can set out from the observation that all income earned is apportioned between wages and profits after the fractions owed to the public and foreign sectors have been deducted. Therefore:

$$\Omega_t + Z_t + F_t + T_t = 1 \qquad (5.1)$$

where Ω and Z are the portions appropriated to wages and profits respectively, T is the portion payable to the public sector and F the portion of income appropriated by the 'rest of the world', i.e. the net cost of imports. Rowthorn then assumes that the portions respectively absorbed by the public and foreign sectors are both exogenously determined, so that the portion that remains available for the private sector is a part R of the income such that:

$$R_t = 1 - \overline{T}_t - \overline{F}_t \qquad (5.2)$$

The income portion appropriated to wages depends on the degree of *aggressiveness* with which unions bargain for higher wages, which is in turn influenced both by the trend in labour demand and, consequently (given the assumption that no increases in output can be achieved with employment remaining constant), by the trend in aggregate demand (D). One further assumption inherent in the model is that wage levels are negotiated at the beginning of each period of time (for instance each year) and do not change within one and the same period.

Therefore the hypothesis to be tested is that the income portion appropriated to wages at the end of a wage bargaining process increases in proportion to demand:

$$\Omega_t^n = f(D_t) \qquad \text{with } f' > 0 \qquad (5.3)$$

where n reflects the wage increase negotiated. Unions bargain for money wages, but as the initial assumption is stable prices, their wage claims are referred to a *real wage target*.[1]

Equation (5.3) has been defined for $D > 0$. Due to the assumption that the portion appropriated to wages will never equal the total income portion available for the private sector, it has an asymptote on the ordinate for $\Omega^n = R$. Thus the possibility that profits are zero or negative is excluded right from the start. In graphic terms what has been said can be represented in Figure 5.1.

As capitalists are assumed to aim at larger profits when demand for commodities is high,[2] also their claims on the income available for the private sector are linked to the trend in aggregate demand.

$$Z_t^* = g(D_t) \qquad \text{with } g' > 0 \qquad (5.4)$$

where the asterisk indicates that Z is the target profit portion.

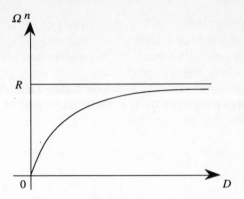

Figure 5.1   *Real wages target and aggregate demand*

Equation (5.4) is similar to (5.3): it has been defined for $D > 0$ and has an asymptote for $Z^* = R - S$, but in this case S is the portion corresponding to subsistence wages.

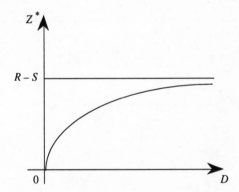

Figure 5.2   *The profit target and aggregate demand*

However, the negotiated profits portion is also determined by the result of the wage bargaining process:

$$Z_t^n = 1 - T_t - F_t - \Omega_t^n = R_t - \Omega_t^n \tag{5.5}$$

Consequently, substituting (5.3) into (5.5) we have:

$$Z_t^n = R_t - f(D_t) \tag{5.6}$$

which clearly shows that Z^n is the complement of Ω^n for R.

The foregoing has been graphically represented in Figure 5.3. Figure 5.1 has been reproduced in sector (a); the complementary relation between Ω^n and Z^n has been reproduced in sector (b); in sector (c) we have used the traditional procedure for transferring the variable onto the ordinate; the inverse relationship between the negotiated profit portion and aggregate demand has been obtained in sector (d).

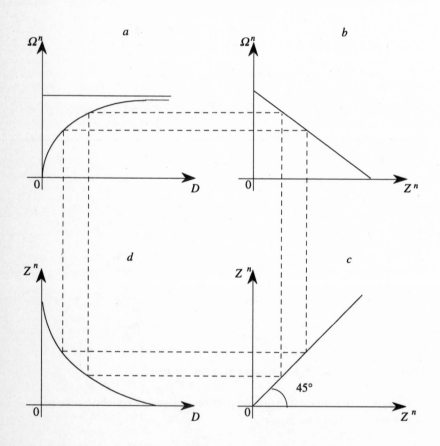

Figure 5.3   The negotiated profit portion

At this point the question is: what will happen if the profit portion actually negotiated falls short of the one originally aimed at? The reaction of capitalists will be to fill the gap by increasing prices – so that it is reasonable to assume that they will more easily be persuaded to grant the workers' wage claims since they know they can achieve their profit target by raising prices.[3] Thus we can write the following equation for the inflation rate:

$$\dot{p}_t = \alpha\left(Z_t^* - Z_t^n\right) \qquad (5.7)$$

$0 \le \alpha \le 1$ is a parameter which measures the pace at which firms achieve their profit target. For the sake of simplicity, in the following pages we will assume that $\alpha = 1$, i.e. that firms tend to achieve their profit target within a single period of time.

Substituting (5.4) and (5.6) into (5.7), we obtain:

$$\dot{p}_t = g\left(D_t\right) - \left[R_t - f\left(D_t\right)\right] \qquad (5.8)$$

and from this:

$$\dot{p}_t = \phi\left(D_t\right) - R_t \qquad (5.9)$$

where $\phi(D) = g(D) + f(D)$; and from (5.9) we directly obtain:

$$\dot{p}_t \lessgtr 0 \qquad \text{if } \phi(D) \gtrless R \qquad (5.10)$$

Equation (5.10) shows the link between the trend in demand and the inflation rate.

The above can be graphically represented based on Figure 5.4. The functions (5.4) and (5.6) have been reported in Figure 5.4 in order to show what correlations there are between the 'aspiration gap' and the aggregate demand level. For example, if aggregate demand equals the segment $0A$, the negotiated profit portion equals the target profit portion; conversely, if demand is equal to $0B$, there will be a gap, FK, between the target portion (FB) and the one actually negotiated (KB). Figure 5.5 clearly highlights that the trend in inflation will be the steeper, the greater the gap between the two portions. At point E in Figure 5.4 the rate of inflation is zero; at higher income and aggregate demand levels it will be a positive value, but at lower levels there will be a deflationary trend.

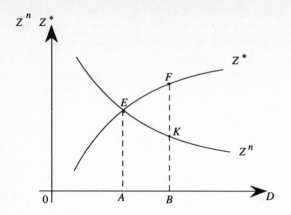

Figure 5.4   The aspiration gap

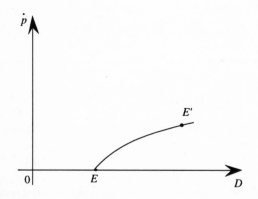

Figure 5.5   The aspiration gap and inflation

The relationship between inflation and unemployment that can be derived from (5.12) is the 'Phillips curve' à la Rowthorn. In point of fact, from what was stated at the beginning of this section we know that the inflation rate, u, is:

$$u = u(D) \qquad (5.11)$$

obviously with $u' < 0$; and from (5.11) we obtain:

$$D = u^{-1}(u) \qquad (5.12)$$

When this is substituted into (5.9), we have:

$$\dot{p}_t = \phi\left[u^{-1}(u_t)\right] - R_t \qquad (5.13)$$

which can be written as follows:

$$\dot{p}_t = h(u_t) \qquad\qquad h' = 0 \qquad (5.14)$$

Equation 5.14 can be represented in the following way (Figure 5.6).

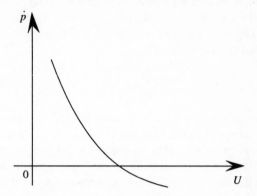

Figure 5.6   The Phillips curve of Rowthorn

But what is the aggregate demand level determined by according to Rowthorn? Here the model acquires 'monetarist' overtones. As a matter of fact, in it the dynamics of aggregate demand and employment is determined by money because Rowthorn assumes that changes in income and employment are brought about by variations in money supply. One possible explanation of the mechanism which sparks off inflation in such a macroeconomic system has been described in Figure 5.7.

As is indicated by arrow 1, monetary demand is influenced by the policies framed by monetary authorities; arrow 2 indicates that any change in monetary demand immediately affects both income and employment. Increases in income and employment in turn heighten social conflict (arrow 3) and this pushes up prices (arrow 4). Arrow 5 points to a 'feedback effect', whereby the rise in prices cancels the original increase in income at least in part, as we will show here below.

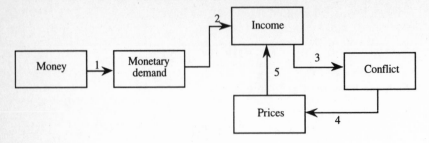

Figure 5.7   Money, conflict and inflation

The first two steps of the Rowthorn model are visibly similar to those of the monetarists because demand rises as a result of an expansion in monetary aggregates. Thus we can write the following version of the quantitative theory of money:

$$\dot{m}_t = \dot{p}_t + \dot{x}_t \tag{5.15}$$

where $\dot{m}_t$ is the rate of growth in money supply and $\dot{x}_t$ is the rate of change in income; no term reflects circulation velocity since this is assumed to be constant. It goes without saying that given a value of $\dot{m}_t$ (exogenously determined), the rise in prices will be inversely proportional to that in income.[4] And if it is assumed that the changes in the variables on the right of the equals sign are caused by changes in money supply, it is these that spark off the above-mentioned conflicting distribution mechanisms whereby the effects of increased money supply will generate a certain price and income effect pattern.

5.3   THE ROWTHORN MODEL WITH ADAPTIVE EXPECTATIONS

So far the Rowthorn model has been illustrated in a version without inflation expectations; this is justified by the fact that on the authority of other economists[5] Rowthorn assumes that price expectations play no role whatsoever at least as long as the inflation rate remains below a given threshold. However, as soon as this threshold value is exceeded, expectations become a decisive element in the inflationary process and the Phillips trade-off is found to change role and significance.

Allowing for expectations – which are assumed to be the same in capitalists and workers – (5.9) must be written as follows:

$$\dot{p}_t = \phi\left(D_t\right) - R_t + \dot{p}_t^e \tag{5.16}$$

where $\dot{p}_t^e$ is the expected rate of change in prices. In place of (5.13) we have to write:

$$\dot{p}_t = \Omega\left[u^{-1}\left(u_t\right)\right] - R_t + \dot{p}_t^e \tag{5.17}$$

i.e.:

$$\dot{p}_t = h\left(u_t\right) + \dot{p}_t^e \tag{5.18}$$

Accordingly, when the relation between unemployment and inflation shown in Figure 5.6 is referred to a model with expectations concerning inflation, it is only applicable to one given value of expected inflation, whilst the short-term Phillips curve is shifted upwards as soon as the value of $\dot{p}_t^e$ increases. The kind of assumption made with respect to the mechanism that generates expectations is crucial to the interpretation of (5.16) and (5.18). If expectations arise in line with the 'adaptive expectations' perspective (as Rowthorn assumed in 1977), in periods of rising inflation the Phillips trade-off will be shifted upwards in each successive period of time and, as a result of this, an ever more accelerating inflationary trend will be sparked off every time the unemployment rate falls below the level at which the claims of both classes are compatible with the income available.

Within a long-term perspective, therefore, the Phillips curve becomes vertical when the threshold below which expectations concerning inflation are irrelevant is exceeded.

What has been discussed so far has been graphically represented in Figure 5.8.

As long as the inflation rate remains below $\dot{p}°$, the Phillips trade-off also holds in a long-term perspective, but as soon as this threshold value is exceeded the relation becomes vertical at the unemployment level at which the claims of the two classes do not result in excessive *expectations*. The question to be raised at this point is whether there is any room for social conflict in a situation where a rising trend in inflation is anticipated.

In this section this question will be answered based on Rowthorn's 1977 model. In the next section we will examine it in more general terms and propose a model which is a re-elaborated version of Rowthorn's.

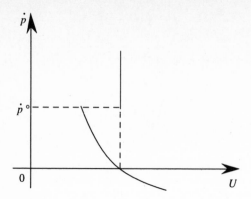

Figure 5.8   The expectation's mechanism in Rowthorn's interpretation

Let us assume that expectations arise through the simplest adaptive mechanism or, more precisely, let us assume expectations be 'static', so that the rate of inflation anticipated for time t equals the inflation rate registered in the previous period of time.[6]

$$\dot{p}_t^e = \dot{p}_{t-1} \tag{5.19}$$

Substituting (5.19) into (5.18) we have:

$$\dot{p}_t = h\ (u) + \dot{p}_{t-1} \tag{5.20}$$

and therefore:

$$\dot{p}_t - \dot{p}_{t-1} = h\left(u_t\right) \tag{5.21}$$

Equation (5.21) highlights a correlation between changes in the inflation and unemployment rates. Graphically, (5.21) can be plotted as a Phillips curve with changes in the inflation rate marked on the ordinate, as shown in Figure 5.9.

This 'new' Phillips curve is based on the acceleration assumption: the inflation rate increases when unemployment is less than 0A, but when unemployment reaches a level greater than 0A, inflation decreases (whilst prices usually do not). As a result of the correlation between money and inflation discussed above, the monetary authorities will succeed in reducing unemployment to a level below 0A only if they are prepared to finance an accelerating inflationary surge.

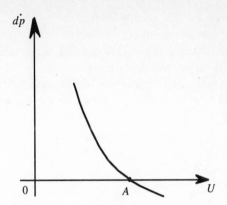

Figure 5.9 The accelerationist hypothesis

From this perspective, social conflict is sparked off by high demand and the manners and causal mechanisms whereby it determines a rise in inflation are those already analysed for the model without expectations.

5.4 A MODEL *À LA* ROWTHORN WITH RATIONAL EXPECTATIONS

Two aspects of the Rowthorn model are worth discussing more thoroughly. First of all it will be interesting to determine if higher levels of conflict can affect 'conflictual parameters' in such a way as to shift the Phillips curve or modify its shape.[7] Subsequently we will also try to establish what effects the introduction of rational expectations has on the Rowthorn model.

The model we are going to use in this section is a partially modified Rowthorn model which makes it easier to examine these issues thoroughly.

Let the system be a 'closed' economy with no public sector. In such a case all the income produced would be apportioned between wages and profits and – as mentioned in the previous paragraph – inflation would be caused by the gap between the target profit portion and the portion actually negotiated.

$$\dot{p}_t = Z_t^* - Z_t^n \qquad (5.22)$$

The target portion can be expressed as a function of the change in income, as in the following equation:

$$Z_t^* = a + b\dot{x}_t \tag{5.23}$$

The parameter a measures the influence of 'structural' factors on the business operators target portion of profits.

An expression reflecting the portion of profits actually negotiated can also be written as a function of the rate of change in income. Indeed, if:

$$\Omega_t^n = c + d\dot{x}_t$$

and bearing in mind that:

$$\Omega^n + Z^n = 1$$

we obtain:

$$Z_t^n = g - d\dot{x}_t \tag{5.24}$$

where $g = 1 - c$, the parameter c stands for the structural elements which influence the wage bargaining process and accordingly the parameter g reflects the target wage portion that workers tend to claim based on what might be defined the 'structural' elements inherent in the power relations between classes.

Equations (5.23) and (5.24) are only defined within one precise interval, $\dot{x}_t = 0$, because linearization, being referred to portions, is admissible only in respect of moderately high values of $\dot{x}_t$ provided these are not too high.

The model is completed by the quantitative equation of money, i.e. (5.15), which for reasons of convenience can be re-written as follows:

$$\dot{m}_t = \dot{p}_t + \dot{x}_t$$

The solutions for $\dot{p}_t$ and $\dot{x}_t$ obtained from this model are as follows:

$$\dot{p}_t = \frac{a + c - 1}{1 + b + d} + \frac{b + d}{1 + b + d} \cdot \dot{m}_t \tag{5.25}$$

$$\dot{x}_t = \frac{1 - a - c}{1 + b + d} + \frac{1}{1 + b + d} \cdot \dot{m}_t \tag{5.26}$$

The foregoing shows that both the inflation rate and increases in income are influenced by the rate of growth in monetary aggregates. In this connection let us mention that an increase in money supply will drive up inflation and income to extents which depend on the values of the parameters a, b, c, d. If the value of $\dot{m}_t$ is assumed to be given, the resulting inflation rate will be determined by the values of a, b, c and d. However, in a model à la Rowthorn increasing levels of social conflict are bound to affect the values of the 'conflictual' parameters. The sign of the price derivatives of a and c shows that any increase in these parameters – with other parameters remaining unchanged – pushes up inflation as a result of higher levels of conflict sparked off by non-economic causes:

$$\frac{\partial \dot{p}_t}{\partial a} = \frac{\partial \dot{p}_t}{\partial c} = \frac{1}{1+b+d} > 0$$

The price derivatives for the parameters b and d are positive if $\dot{m}_t > (a+c-1)$ and negative if $\dot{m}_t < (a+c-1)$:

$$\frac{\partial \dot{p}_t}{\partial b} = \frac{\partial \dot{p}_t}{\partial d} = \frac{\dot{m}_t - (a+c-1)}{(1+b+d)^2}$$

The latter result indicates that when the rate of increase in $\dot{m}_t$ is smaller than the structural gap between the target profit and that actually achieved after the negotiation process, a greater reactivity of these portions to changes in income ends up by slowing down inflation. Thus the Phillips curve is shifted upwards or downwards whenever social conflict mounts as a result of historical and/or institutional causes, rather than due to 'the market mechanism'; and this occurs because the target portions change irrespective of changes in demand, i.e. due to rises in the parameters a and c. And the slope of the Phillips curve will become more or less steep depending on the impact of demand on the target portions concerned, i.e. on changes in the parameters b and d.

At this point we will discuss the second problem raised at the beginning of this section, namely what changes are observed in the Rowthorn model as soon as rational expectations are taken into account.

As mentioned in the previous section, the Rowthorn model is based on the idea that expectations concerning inflation play a significant role whenever the inflationary process approaches a certain degree of intensity. Today this widely shared assumption seems to highlight the reason why a phase in history in which flexible real money wages associated with rising prices enabled the economic system to achieve higher levels of employment was followed by a phase in which this result is no longer attainable because the era of monetary illusion is a thing of the past.[8]

Thus Rowthorn's assumption of an adaptive expectations mechanism stems in part from the particular period in which he wrote his article and in part from much more fundamental reasons.[9] The literature on expectations has highlighted a number of theoretical shortcomings in the 'adaptive approach': among them an ample scope for systematic errors and non-rational behaviour on the part of economic agents when expectations concerning inflation are exclusively based on past price increases.

Accordingly it may be interesting to ascertain to what extent our conclusions in sections 5.2 and 5.3 will change as soon as rational expectations are introduced. This point also has a bearing on the role conflict is found to play in Rowthorn's model when his 'monetarist' reflections are further developed and the assumption that expectations are formed in a rational manner is taken into account.

Returning to the previous model, (5.22) becomes:

$$\dot{p}_t = Z_t^* - Z_t^n + E(\dot{p}_t) \tag{5.27}$$

or, taking into account (5.23) and (5.24):

$$\dot{p}_t = (a-g) + (b+d)\ \dot{x}_t + E(\dot{p}_t) \tag{5.28}$$

Adding the quantitative equation and a money supply rule equation, we obtain:

$$\dot{x}_t = \dot{m}_t - \dot{p}_t \tag{5.15}$$

$$\dot{m}_t = \overline{\dot{m}}_t + \varepsilon_t \tag{5.29}$$

Equation (5.29) reflects Rowthorn's assumption that money supply decisions *precede* the causal process from which conflict and inflation both stem: in point of fact it is assumed that monetary aggregates grow at a rate $\dot{m}_t$ plus the causal shock ε, which has the usual properties – mean value 0 and variance σ^2.

Solving the model for $\dot{p}_t$, and considering expectations to be exogenous, we obtain:[10]

$$\dot{p}_t = \frac{a-g}{1+b+d} + \frac{b+d}{1+b+d} \cdot \left(\overline{\dot{m}}_t + \varepsilon_t\right) + \frac{1}{1+b+d} \cdot E\left(\dot{p}_t\right) \tag{5.30}$$

To calculate the anticipated value of $\dot{p}$ we substitute the expected values of the three variables and then solve the equation. Thus we have:

$$E\left(\dot{p}_t\right) = \overline{\dot{m}}_t + \frac{a-g}{b+d} \tag{5.31}$$

Substituting (5.31) into (5.30), the result is:

$$\dot{p}_t = \overline{\dot{m}}_t + \frac{a-g}{b+d} + \frac{b+d}{1+b+d} \cdot \varepsilon_t \tag{5.32}$$

$$\dot{x}_t = -\frac{a-g}{b+d} + \frac{1}{1+b+d} \cdot \varepsilon_t \tag{5.33}$$

Equations (5.32) and (5.33) clearly highlight the effects produced by the introduction of rational expectations into the Rowthorn model: the inflation–unemployment trade-off is no longer valid – the economy departs from the 'natural' rate of unemployment only because of the stochastic component of money supply[11] – and monetary authorities are prevented from performing the role of 'conflict mediators' the original Rowthorn model seemed to vest in them.

At given values of the rate of change in monetary aggregates, the system is thrown off balance by each change in the parameters a and g (where, it should be remembered, $g = 1 - c$). More precisely, the moment when the gap between a and g widens, the rate of inflation soars and equilibrium income falls, whereupon the so-called vertical Phillips curve is shifted toward the origin of the axes:[12] in Figure 5.10 the rate of increase in income declines from $0B$ to $0C$. A higher value of b weakens the impact of the gap between a and g on inflation and, at the same time, strengthens the effect of the stochastic component of money supply on prices.

At this point we note that the effects of substituting rational for adaptive expectations in the Rowthorn model are in part comparable to those which arise in a neoclassical model, but as soon as we rewrite the model in a manner which makes it possible for conflict to exert its influence also through factors other than demand, we reach the interesting conclusion that while the unemployment–inflation trade-off disappears, mounting social conflict keeps undermining the equilibrium of the system. And this may explain why the Rowthorn model is still at the forefront of the continuing debate between neoclassical and Keynesian theories of inflation and unemployment.

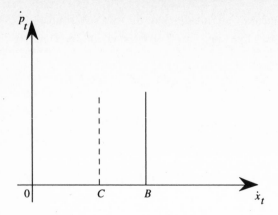

Figure 5.10   NRU and conflict

5.5   A PHILLIPS CURVE WITH KALECKIAN CHARACTERISTICS

The attempt to found a relation *à la* Phillips on the conflict over income distribution can be considered a further re-elaboration of a pioneer idea of Kalecki's. In a well-known 1943 essay entitled 'Political Aspects of Full Employment', Kalecki pointed out that it was the conflictual relations between classes that prevented capitalism from reconciling full employment with price stability: in a full-employment system, he argued, workers tend to claim increasingly higher wages because the factors which normally weaken their contractual power are missing (see Kalecki, 1943b, p. 168).

> Indeed, under a regime of permanent full employment, the 'sack' would cease to play its role as a disciplinary measure. The social position of the boss would be undermined, and the self-assurance and class-consciousness of the working class would grow. Strikes for wage increases and improvements of conditions of work would create political tension (Kalecki, 1943, p. 351).

In many advanced capitalist countries, those elements that in Kalecki's 1943 article had been presented as obstacles to full employment actually proved to be the long run *effects* of policies designed to achieve the full employment objective in many capitalist economies: for instance the wage hike that exploded in the 1970s was often explained as the inevitable result of growing worker and union power during the two decades of rapid economic growth which followed upon World War II. As a result, in more recent years Kalecki's essay found itself the focus of massive interest from economists as a lucid anticipation of the inflationary spiral entailed in the full-employment objective and as a possible theoretic basis for the Phillips curve (see Salvati, 1981).

Even more recently the link between the Phillips curve and the macroeconomic theory of this Polish economist has been approached from a different perspective which focuses on different elements in his contribution (see Myatt, 1986; Musella, 1988b).

It is a fact that those wishing to approach the economic process from a non-neoclassical perspective which would account for the impact of social conflict upon the system will find in Kalecki's economic thinking a very solid basis for their attempt.[13] And this is why it may be interesting to test the inverse *unemployment–inflation* relation against the background of Kalecki's thought by further developing a well-known analytical formulation of the income and distribution theory inspired by the contribution of this Polish Marxist economist.[14]

However, before we start examining Kalecki's macroeconomic model it will be convenient to discuss the gap between workers' wage claims and the wages offered by firms. As we know, workers often have a given target real wage (B), so that:

$$W = BP \qquad (5.34)$$

where W is the money wage and P the level of proces, while firms fix prices based on the *mark-up*. Assuming, for the sake of simplicity, that direct costs only include labour costs, we have:

$$P = \frac{(1+v)\,W}{\pi} \qquad (5.35)$$

Thus the real wage offered is:

$$\frac{W}{P} = \frac{\pi}{1+v} \qquad (5.36)$$

At this point we assume that wages are adjusted immediately, while price adjustments lag behind by one period of time:

$$W_t = B \cdot P_t \qquad (5.37)$$

$$P_t = \frac{(1+v)\ W_{t-1}}{\pi} \qquad (5.38)$$

The results we obtain as soon as this hypothesis is introduced diverge greatly from those of the Rowthorn model: it is workers that manage to attain their target wage, whilst the income of profit-earners is a residual value determined by an endogenous process (which means that firms are unable to bring prices immediately into line with the increase in wages).

Assuming the 'degree of monopoly' to be given and labour productivity to be constant, the result is an increasing relation between the target real wage and the inflation rate reflected by the following equation:[15]

$$\dot{p}_t = \frac{1+v}{\pi}B - 1 \qquad (5.39)$$

This relation (5.39) has been represented in Figure 5.15: the inflation rate increases in proportion to the target wage; the function has an intercept for $B = \pi/(1+v)$ because the inflation rate is zero when the value of the target wage is exactly matched by the wage offered.

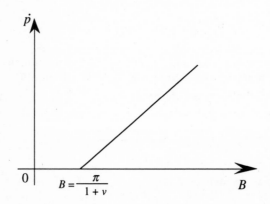

Figure 5.11   The real wage and inflation

Before we can plot the Phillips curve we have to write the fundamental equations of the Kaleckian macroeconomic model in order to investigate the relations between workers' asked wage rate and the employment level:

$$X = C_w + C_c + I \qquad (5.40)$$

$$C_w = \frac{W}{P} \cdot L \tag{5.41}$$

$$C_c = A + \alpha \ \frac{R}{P} \tag{5.42}$$

$$R = Y - WL \tag{5.43}$$

$$I = \bar{I} \tag{5.44}$$

$$L = \frac{X}{\pi} \tag{5.45}$$

$$Y = P \cdot X \tag{5.46}$$

Equation (5.40) bears out the fact that aggregate demand is the sum of workers' consumption expenditure plus capitalists' consumption and investment expenditure; (5.41) is based on the assumption that workers spend all their income on consumer goods; (5.42) is the equation for capitalists' consumption.Equation (5.43) reflects the hypothesis that all income is appropriated to wages and profits; (5.44) that investment expenditure is exogenously determined. Equation (5.45) expresses the amount of labour employed as the relation between total output and average labour productivity; (5.46) defines monetary income as equal to real income multiplied by the price level.

From the system of equations (5.40–5.46) we may derive an expression which establishes a relationship between the equilibrium level of income and the autonomous components of demand, distributive variables and propensity toward saving:

$$X = \frac{1}{P - \frac{W}{\pi}} \cdot \frac{P(I+A)}{1-\alpha} \tag{5.47}$$

The quantity of labour employed by the system is easily calculated based on (5.47):

$$L = \frac{1+v}{v} \cdot \frac{I+A}{\pi(1-\alpha)} \tag{5.48}$$

At this point let z be the *mark-up* actually teached: it differs from v because capitalists' price adjustments lag behind by one period of time. From (5.37), considering:

$$P_t = \frac{(1+z)W_t}{\pi} \qquad (5.49)$$

we obtain:

$$z = \frac{\pi}{B} - 1 \qquad (5.50)$$

and, substituting z for v in (5.48), we have:

$$L = \frac{1}{\pi - B} \cdot \frac{I+A}{1-\alpha} \qquad (5.51)$$

with

$$\frac{\partial L}{\partial B} = \frac{1}{(\pi - B)^2} \cdot \frac{I+A}{1-\alpha} > 0$$

From (5.51) we deduce that the amount of labour employed by the system increases in proportion to the rise in the target wage of workers.

From the above it follows that – contrary to the principles of classical economy – an increase in wages, which is the result of greater union power, increases employment, while a fall in wages, which is the result of a lesser contractual power on the part of unions, reduces employment. As unions grow weaker during periods of depression and are prevented from opposing wage cuts effectively, this weakness actually drives up unemployment instead of reducing it (Kalecki, 1971, p. 102).[16]

The relation expressed by (5.51) has been represented in Figure 5.12 and is seen to rise at an incresing rate because the value of L increases more than proportionally to the increase in B. The reason why this relation deserves being examined in even greater detail is that it qualifies the resulting Phillips curve as 'Kaleckian'. In it the increases in income and employment are clearly the effect, while the higher wage rates demanded are the cause: profits decline as the wage rate rises, so that aggregate demand for consumption goods will also increase as a result of income redistribution and the resulting rise in aggregate demand and the equilibrium income level will in turn boost employment figures.

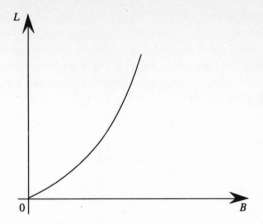

Figure 5.12   The real wage and employment

Useless to say, the assumption that price adjustments lag behind by one period of time while wages are immediately adjusted is of the utmost importance. Failing this, any increase in money wages would be immediately offset by price increases and, as could easily be shown, neither income redistribution nor any variation in employment levels will ensue.

At this point it will be enough to add an inverse relationship between the quantity of labour employed and the unemployment rate to obtain an unemployment–inflation relation founded on a Kaleckian model:

$$U = f(L) \qquad\qquad f' = 0 \qquad (5.52)$$

For the sake of greater clarity, we can plot the functions which result in the inverse inflation–unemployment relationship in a single graph with four quadrants (Figure 5.13). The first quadrant reproduces Figure 5.11; the second shows the relation between the wage rate demanded by workers and the employment level, whilst the third presents the inverse relationship between the quantity of labour employed and the unemployment level reflected in equation (5.52). Consequently the fourth quadrant can be used to represent the inverse inflation–unemployment relationship with the typical declining slope of the Phillips curve.[17]

To explain this finding, let us start from a real wage level equal to $0H$; in the first quadrant we identify a point A on the function which links the inflation level to workers' asked wage rate and which is a point at which the inflation rate is $0T$. The employment level $0M$, which corresponds to the wage rate $0H$, is obtained by projecting point A into the second quadrant. As a result of relation (5.54), in the third quadrant $0M$ corresponds to a precise unemployment level, $0Q$. Plotting this unemployment level in the fourth quadrant we obtain a point, G, which is the inflation-unemployment combination associated to the real wage $0T$. If the whole process is reiterated with a different value for workers' asked wage rate, we obtain an inverse relationship between unemployment and inflation which is precisely the Kaleckian Phillips curve.

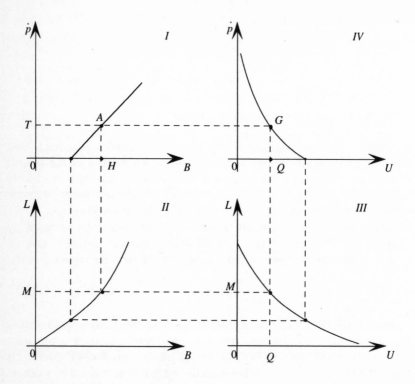

Figure 5.13 A Kaleckian Phillips curve

5.6 ON KALECKI'S THEORY AND THE PHILLIPS CURVE

The above statement that the theoretical basis on which a Kaleckian Phillips curve of Figure 5.13 can be plotted is equation (5.51) in quadrant II requires further qualification.

The Kaleckian Phillips curve must be interpreted as based on non-traditional causal links: if the mark-up and growth in productivity are given, a rise in wages 'causes', at the same time, a rise in prices; but through the redistribution of income to the benefit of workers it also drives up employment.

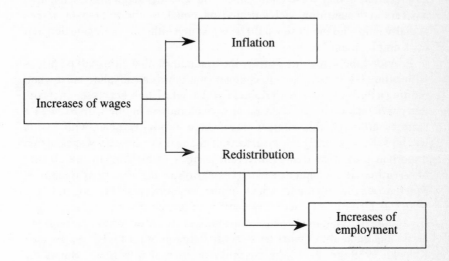

Figure 5.14   Kaleckian model and the Phillips curve

As can be seen from Figure 5.14, it is not low unemployment levels that push up wages and prices by conferring more power on unions, nor is it higher wages that bring down unemployment in line with the hypotheses underlying job search literature; here it is the growth in money wages that push up inflation on the one hand and drive down unemployment levels on the other.[18] Furthermore, increases in money wages are linked to the desire of workers to earn higher real wages and the difficulty firms find in promptly responding to wage increases. Thus we may argue that while in Rowthorn's approach conflict is explained based on the Phillips curve, in Myatt's approach conflict is an exogenous phenomenon and the inverse relationship between unemployment and inflation arises as a result of the macroeconomic relations underlying the model as soon as an exogenous impulse generates a rise in money wages. The main cause of increases in income and employment is workers' lower propensity to save as compared to capitalists' – a hypothesis implying that both aggregate expenditure and employment are found to increase when income is redistributed to the benefit of the former.

As mentioned above, the existence of the Phillips curve is closely associated with the idea that workers (i.e. unions) are in a position to oblige firms to cut their actual mark-ups (though not their target profits as well). This means that there is a reason, whether economic or institutional, which prevents firms from adjusting prices presently and enables workers to obtain immediate benefits.[19] Failing this, income would not be redistributed as a result of higher wage claims and – since in the model proposed above workers' consumption is by definition equal to the aggregate wages actually paid – no increase would be registered either in aggregate demand or in employment levels.

Provided the foregoing is true, the assumption that firms adjust prices with a time lag as compared to changes in wages is an absolute must when plotting a Phillips curve with Kaleckian characteristics. On closer analysis, this curve may be justified based on considerations in line with Kalecki's theories although this subject is nowhere explicitly dealt with in his writings. Kalecki analyses the effects of changes in monetary wages in two important essays written in different periods of his life. In the closing observations to a chapter of his 1939 *Essays in the Theory of Economic Fluctuations*, following an attack on the 'supporters of this slogan (rigid wages as a source of unemployment) who preach that by making wages rigid collective bargaining causes unemployment and poverty in the working class' and encourages workers to cease bargaining for higher wages (see Kalecki, 1939, pp. 38–9), he raises the problem that workers' claims for higher wages may become pointless if each step is counterbalanced by a rise in the cost of living. But his answer to this question is no, since changes in real wages, though smaller than those in money wages, may well be fairly substantial (Kalecki, 1939, p. 40).

In point of fact Kalecki's 1939 paper links up with Keynesian criticisms of the neoclassical theory of the flexibility of wages and employment, but as in this paper Kalecki specifically addresses the hypothesis of a fall in money wages, he fails to give attention to the link between rises in money wages and changes in real wages.

The last article in which Kalecki concerned himself in detail with the effects of wage increases was published posthumously (Kalecki, 1971, pp. 96–103). It endorses the view that union action may succeed in reducing profit margins and achieving the redistribution of income to the benefit of workers because in some cases, firms have difficulty in increasing prices proportionally to the wage hike.

Kalecki's argument can be illustrated based on the price equation he used in his 1971 essay, namely:

$$\frac{P-C}{C}=f\left(\frac{\overline{P}}{P}\right) \qquad \text{with } f' > 0 \qquad (5.53)$$

where $C = W/\pi$, and by quoting his arguments on the subject (Kalecki, 1971):

> To sum up, trade union power restrains the mark-ups (...) Now, this power manifests itself in the scale of wage rises demanded and achieved. If an increase of bargaining capacity is demonstrated by spectacular achievements, there is a downward shift in functions $f\left(\overline{P}/P\right)$ and the mark-ups decline. A redistribution of national income from profits to wages will then take place. But this redistribution is much smaller than that which would be obtained if prices were stable. The rise in wages is to a great extent 'shifted to consumers' (Kalecki, 1971, pp. 100-01).

In the above quote Kalecki maintains that price adjustments following upon wage increases are only partial. However, this partial adjustment may be traced back to the time lag which elapses before this adjustment is made: in his opinion, in an economic system with non-competitive markets this is one of the ways in which a growth in union power may reduce the degree of monopoly (see Sawyer, 1985, pp. 109 and 113).

Doubtlessly the subsequent adjustment in prices can indicate that firms, being dissatisfied with the profit margins they have actually earned, are trying to streamline income distribution in line with their wishes but are unable to achieve this aim so long as workers retain the advantage of adjusting their wages promptly. As the conditions prevailing in commodities markets prevent firms from adjusting prices if not after a certain time lag, also their attempt to restore the income distribution that was knocked off balance by the relevant wage increases must necessarily fail. But how do these conditions work?

The time lag with which prices are adjusted can be explained based on at least two different arguments: the climate of uncertainty in which firms make their pricing decisions and the constraints stemming from international competition.

With respect to the first of these arguments, let us assume that firms operating in an oligopolistic markets base their pricing decisions on the expected behaviour of other firms and let us also assume that the information firms have access to is not enough to establish if, and to what extent, wage pressures comparable to that to which it is subject are widespread in the economic system as a whole. In such a situation a firm conducting business within an oligopolistic market, fearing to lose market shares by increasing its prices, will put up with lower mark-ups in the period of time considered, but in the subsequent period it will raise its prices since the wage increases concerned will be found to have been obtained in the system as a whole.

This argument can be illustrated by reference to Kalecki's last formulation of the price theory, based on equation (5.53).[20] Suitably transformed, this can be re-written as:

$$P = C \left[1 + f \left(\frac{\bar{P}}{P} \right) \right] \qquad (5.54)$$

To support the view that the firm bases its pricing decision on expectations concerning the behaviour of other firms, we further modify (5.54) as follows:

$$P_t = C \left\{ 1 + f \left[\frac{E\left(\bar{P}_t\right)}{P} \right] \right\} \qquad (5.55)$$

If – in the simplest-case scenario – we assume that the representative agent expects other firms to leave prices stable, we obtain that:

$$E\left(\bar{P}_t\right) = \bar{P}_{t-1}$$

Any rise in C will lower the function f, as $\bar{P}$ does not increase in proportion to P; if all firms make the same error in their forecasts, in the short run the rise in the price index will lag behind the increase in wages. The second characteristic of the commodities market that may impede adjusting prices simultaneously with rises in wages is linked to international competition. If firms are assumed to operate in a world-wide market where they have to cope with global competition, they cannot pass wage increases onto prices without running the risk of losing substantial market shares. Studies by Sylos Labini focused attention on this point, supporting the hypothesis of a late adjustment of prices to wages with evidence provided by numerous empirical estimates for several industrial countries. Sylos Labini explained this time lag with constraints stemming from international competition. In his earliest studies he analysed periods with fixed exchange rates, while in later studies he also tested this hypothesis for periods with flexible exchange rates (see Sylos Labini, 1974, 1984).

Experience has shown that in a system with flexible exchange rates, above all in countries strongly dependent on international trade, the central bank delays reductions of the exchange rate and at times even tries to avoid money devaluation. As a result, firms find it difficult to pass cost increases onto prices. In so doing central banks are doubtlessly guided by the fear of sparking off a 'nasty devaluation/inflation spiral'.

Kalecki's price equation (1971) can also be used to illustrate the second argument. Let us re-write (5.54):

$$P = C\left[1 + f\left(\frac{\overline{P}}{P}\right)\right]$$

To obtain the aggregation level required for our purpose, let us interpret P as the general price level prevailing in the manufacturing sector and $\overline{P}$ as the price index registered in a number of countries competing with one another. If a wage rate increases more than proportionally to the trend in productivity it will push up the value of C, but in the absence of changes in the international situation it will also lower the function f and reduce profit margins; domestic prices will not increase in proportion to wages and mark-ups will remain low as a result of greater union power and international competition. Only when monetary authorities consent to devaluate their currency – a measure which firms can be expected to press for – will firms have an opportunity to transfer their higher costs onto prices.

5.7   CONCLUSIONS

The two theories discussed in this chapter are based on reconstructions of the inflation–unemployment trade-off which differ greatly both from each other and from more traditional interpretations of the celebrated curve proposed by Phillips in 1958.

As mentioned before in this chapter, the contributions we are discussing are of a heterodox nature because they either set out from a different link between unemployment and rises of the wage rate (Rowthorn) or suggest different interpretations in terms of the causality links between the variables involved in the Phillips curve (Myatt).

It is likely that the success of the Phillips curve in macroeconomic debates from 1958 to the present stems at least in part from the fact that it encouraged attempts, such as the ones examined above, to find evidence that would support the link between unemployment and the wage hike suggested by the curve.

NOTES

1. Here Rowthorn's approach does not seem to depart from that of other authors of the Cambridge Policy Group (see the essays quoted in footnote 8 of Chapter 4), excepting the hypothesis that the target wage is sensitive to changes in demand. On this point see, also, Lavoie, 1993, pp. 379–82.

2. Here Rowthorn's line of reasoning seems to recall the neoclassical theory of the increasing mark-up. For a demonstration, see Musella, 1988a, pp. 1354–5. An interesting assumption behind the Rowthorn model is the existence of two different 'arenas': the labour market, where an increase in demand strengthens the position of workers (and thus weakens firms); and the commodities market, in which an increase in demand strengthens firms (and weakens consumers). Thus Rowthorn seems to paint a scenario which was very clearly outlined in Scitovski, 1978, pp. 221–33.

3. This argument was endorsed by many Marxist and non-Marxist authors (see, for example, Devine, 1974, pp. 79–92). As argued by Lavoie, this assumption is justified above all when firms think that policy makers are pursuing full employment as their target (see Lavoie, 1993, pp. 389–91).

4. As mentioned before, the Rowthorn model assumes the existence of exogenous money. In this respect it departs noticeably from other conflict-driven inflation models in which money plays an essentially passive role. See the – diverging – opinions expressed on the subject by Hicks (1974) and Weintraub (1978a). For a general discussion of this point, see Musella, 1992b.

5. See, for example, Eckstein and Brinner, 1972.

6. The adaptive expectation assumption simplifies the process without significantly affecting its conclusions, but it may be justified by precise institutional rules such as a wage-indexation scheme.

7. Rowthorn only discusses these aspects in very general terms in a short paragraph dealing with 'structural changes' (see Rowthorn, 1977, pp. 220–5).

8. For a clear and lucid discussion of this thesis, see Giersch, 1987, pp. 35–52.

9. Other authoritative economists from the Cambridge School, for instance Kaldor and Trevithick (1981, p. 15) have proposed a critical view of the rational expectation hypothesis.

10. For a useful procedure to be adopted in solving models with rational expectations, see above, note 7 of Chapter 2.

11. It is worth mentioning that Rowthorn attributes a significantly different meaning to this level of unemployment. 'In conventional monetarism $U^°$ is the natural rate of unemployment, which is primarily determined by the competitive and informational structure of the labour market. (...) In the present theory, however, $U^°$ is the level of unemployment at which the claims of the rival parties become mutually consistent. Demand functions as a regulator of class conflict. On the workers' side a low level of demand isolates militants from the mass of the workers and strengthens the hand of moderate leaders against dissenting elements. On the employers' side it reduces their ability to raise prices and may force them to revise downward their target profit margins' (Rowthorn, 1977, p. 237).

12. In the quotation reported in the previous note Rowthorn clearly suggests that the natural rate may be affected by 'exogenous' causes of conflict.

13. For a thorough analysis of Kalecki's thought, see Sawyer, 1985 and Sebastiani, 1985, 1989.

14. See Myatt, 1986, pp. 447–62. This author sets out and further elaborates a model which was proposed by Asimakopulos in a 1975 article (Asimakopulos, 1975, pp. 313–33). The model concerned differs from Asimakopulos' because some of its equations have been simplified in order to bear out more clearly the elements on which a Kaleckian Phillips curve is based.

15. The equations used to determine the inflation rate are specifically Kaleckian because prices are assumed to be adjusted only after a certain period of time. This fact can be explained bearing in mind that when unions claim higher wages they reduce the 'degree of monopoly' because they cut the profit margins actually earned by firms. See Kalecki, 1971; see, also, Asimakopulos, 1980–81, pp. 158–69, who makes it clear that profit margins may also diminish because firms fail to bring their mark up into line with the increase in wages.

16. Once again this argument of Kalecki's concerns the relation between a fall in wages and the employment level. Some years ago a fine essay by Marglin (see Marglin, 1984, pp. 115–44) sparked off an interesting debate on this theme. See, for instance, Nell's criticisms (1985, pp. 173–8) of Marglin's thesis that a reverse relationship between real wages and employment lies at the basis of all the theoretical paradigms of economic science. On this issue, see also Riach, 1995, pp. 163–75.

17. Myatt also discusses the actual meaning of the point at which the Phillips curve intercepts the x-axis in the model presented: 'It is important to note that the horizontal intercept of this "Phillips curve" is not a natural rate of unemployment. In fact it has no relationship

with full employment whatsoever. Its position depends on expectations of income growth and the ability of the system to meet those expectations. It does not depend on the condition of zero excess demand or supply in the labor market which determines the natural rate of unemployment. However, the intercept of our "Phillips curve" may well be a Non Accelerating Inflation Rate of Unemployment (NAIRU)' (Myatt, 1986, p. 457).

18. Thanks to this, also another aspect of the issue which surfaced during the debate over the neoclassical Phillips curve can be accounted for in the non-neoclassical framework. As mentioned above, one conclusion of Friedman's was that the relation between unemployment and rises of the wage rate hike was to be explained by assuming causal links symmetrically opposed to those suggested by Lipsey.

19. Here the difference with respect to the Rowthorn model is apparent: whilst in this model it is capitalists that must, so to speak, put up with the money wages obtained by workers in each period of time, in the model illustrated in Section 5.2 it is workers that have to put up with the prices fixed by firms.

20. On the evolution of Kalecki's pricing theory, see Basile, Salvadori, 1984–85 and Sawyer, 1985, pp. 20–22. For a critical view, see Jossa, 1989.

6 Phillips curve, hysteresis and Keynesian theory

6.1 INTRODUCTION

Summing up the main points made in the previous chapters, here we intend to examine a number of interpretations of the Phillips curve from the perspective of the debate between supporters of the NRU and NAIRU while, at the same time, trying to establish the current state of the debate on the unemployment–inflation trade-off within non-neoclassical approaches to macroeconomics.

Setting out from the distinction between NRU and NAIRU, in Section 2 we will examine the stark opposition between schools up to the late 1980s, throwing light on the different views neoclassical economists and Keynesians have traditionally taken with respect to the way the labour market works.[1] In Sections 6.3–6.5 we will discuss the path dependence of the natural rate of unemployment (or NAIRU) in order to establish to what extent it departs from monetarist approaches to the Phillips curve and marks a decisive return to Keynesian ideas about demand management policies. While the application of the hysteresis theory to the Phillips curve has often been thought to imply a straightforward rebuttal of the relation first propounded in 1958, in Section 6.5 we will try to show that it might in fact be viewed as an attempt to recover the original meaning of the well-known curve which was plotted by Phillips some forty years ago and whose original meaning was often blurred in later approaches excessively tied to the neoclassical tradition.

6.2 NAIRU *VERSUS* NRU

As mentioned in Section 2.5, a major point in monetarist criticisms of the Phillips curve is the argument that a natural rate of unemployment does exist and that it is hardly affected by Keynesian policies of aggregate demand.

In Chapter 2, examining Friedman's stance on the subject we pointed to certain elements, in his definitions, which make it possible to view equilibrium unemployment either as a NAIRU or as a NIRU. However, while the former is by no means an equilibrium point between demand and supply of labour, the latter stems from the tradition of 'natural' equilibria and was thus often presented as a different designation of full employment.[2]

In the previous four chapters we provided sufficient evidence that the NRU is closely associated with neoclassical theory, while the NAIRU has its theoretical basis in the Keynesian and neo-Marxist traditions. Yet in the literature on the Phillips curve this distinction was for many years held to be irrelevant and of no consequence.

One obvious reason for this is that both these approaches accept the idea that the Phillips curve becomes vertical in the long run, a fact which implies a critique of Keynesian demand management policies which undermines Keynesian economics at its very roots.[3]

Another reason which may explain why the NAIRU and NRU are often equated with each other is the fact that it is difficult to distinguish between them in empirical terms. The only way to estimate the equilibrium rate is, in fact, to base the analysis on the trend of the unemployment rate or the mean value of past-year unemployment rates or, even better, to consider the natural rate as 'the residual unemployment after fluctuations directly attributable to business cycles are averaged out' (see Isaac, 1993, p. 458) or the 'unemployment rate consistent with a constant rate of inflation' (Ando and Brayton, 1995, p. 274).[4]

However, neither of these arguments is in itself strong enough to dispel the theoretical distinction between NAIRU and NRU, since in this case more than in any other it is clear that the different designations are not based on different assumptions concerning the way the capitalist system or, more specifically, the labour market works.

In point of fact, when the NAIRU and NIRU concepts were explicitly introduced into literature in the late 1970s, any and whatsoever references to the so-called 'natural' situations of the economic system were dropped and, consequently, any possible misinterpretations of the necessary correspondence between equilibrium level of unemployment and situations of full employment were ruled out once and forever.[5] In spite of this only a handful of theorists argued that the NRU versus NAIRU opposition reflected the conflict between those who maintained that the system tended toward full employment equilibrium (i.e. the NRU theorists) and, conversely, those who conceived of the NAIRU as an equilibrium with involuntary unemployment.

Yet the Keynesian matrix underlying the concept of NAIRU was apparent right from the start. As is well known, right from its earliest interpretations the Phillips Curve was used by some to account for demand–pull inflation and by others to explain cost–push inflation. Those who trace inflation back to the impact of costs ascribe a great role to the power of unions in fixing wage levels and usually explain prices by reference to the full-cost theory. In their interpretation of the Phillips Curve they consequently argue that the higher the level of economic activity, the more prices are pushed up (or prevented from decreasing) from year to year, because decreases in unemployment levels strengthen the bargaining power of labour unions and, in any case, push up wage levels.[6] Any increases in demand and decreases in unemployment strengthen the bargaining power of the working class and unions for a number of reasons which need not be analysed in detail here. It will be enough to say that as the interests of the jobless are in conflict with the interests of those in work, any increase in unemployment hampers the action of trade unions by reducing both their bargaining power and their determination to make use of the power they have.

Even according to this interpretation the relationship between the wage growth rate and unemployment is a decreasing one and eventually intersects the abscissa. But the point concerned is the NAIRU, not the NRU, because it has *nothing* to do with a situation in which demand for labour equals supply and is thus fully compatible with *involuntary* unemployment.

Let us mention that in this approach a decrease in unemployment is assumed to be the cause of wage increases, not vice versa. And this is certainly one of the reasons which lead us to label it as *Keynesian*. A major tenet of Keynesian theory is indeed that employment, far from being determined by wage levels, is actually the element which determines wage levels (see, for instance, Weintraub, 1958, chapter VI and VII; Davidson and Smolensky, 1964, chapter XI; Davidson, 1967 and 1983, Riach, 1995).

As is well known, it is precisely over this issue that the theorists who provided interpretations of the Phillips curve split into two different groups right from the start: some propounded conflicting interpretations mostly based on full cost theory and explained inflation as the result of the pressure of costs, while others suggested interpretations in line with Lipsey's and explained both wage and price increases by reference to the law of demand and supply. At this point, when the NAIRU was discovered it would have been reasonable to assume that the gap between these two opposed groups would further widen, with Keynesians holding the NAIRU to be compatible with involuntary unemployment and neoclassical economists interpreting wage rises as the result of excess demand and the NRU as the rate of unemployment, whether voluntary or frictional, at which demand equals supply of labour.[7]

As it was, from the latter half of the 1980s onwards opposed views concerning the equilibrium rate of unemployment were propounded from a highly different perspective: in fairly traditional approaches the equilibrium rate of unemployment was equated with an employment level which is not influenced by demand management policies;[8] in heterodox macroeconomic approaches, following hysteresis studies which will be discussed in the following sections it was assumed that many equilibrium unemployment rates did exist and that Keynesian policies could effectively influence the rate which was actually reached in each economic system. Consequently, whereas until a few years ago supporters of the NAIRU (excepting some, for instance Myatt, 1986, pp. 457–8) would have agreed on the alleged ineffectiveness of demand policies with respect to equilibrium unemployment,[9] today the scenario has changed and the path dependence of the natural unemployment rate induced Keynesians, Post-Keynesians and Kaleckians to abandon the view that unemployment could only be countered by means of concerted incomes policies and to rethink the positive role played by demand management policies in situations of equilibrium with unemployment.

Accordingly a major step towards correct non-neoclassical theory would be to focus on recent experiences in many countries, which clearly show that there is not just one equilibrium level of unemployment to which the system steadily tends. The actual record of events in Europe in the 1970s and 1980s sharply contradicts the idea of a single unemployment rate at which inflation neither increases nor decreases (see Jenkinson, 1987 and 1990; Juhn et al., 1991, McDonald, 1995, pp. 102–15), both because in past decades persistently high unemployment rates often failed to bring about a permanent decline in inflation and, above all, because in many advanced capitalistic countries the unemployment rate at which inflation was constant has been on the increase over the past years.[10]

6.3   CHANGES IN THE EQUILIBRIUM RATE OF EMPLOYMENT: SOME SUPPORTING EVIDENCE

As was mentioned before, monetarism and the interpretation of the Phillips curve which was suggested by neoclassical economists asserted itself following Friedman's and Phelps' contributions, have one weak point in common, namely the idea of a *natural rate* of unemployment toward which the system should constantly tend spontaneously. At first the NRU hypothesis was enunciated in a fairly radical way, as the NRU was assumed to originate mainly from demographic factors and to be thus fairly constant. As a matter of fact, Friedman never contended that the NRU was the result of persistent, i.e. constant forces; he traced it back to real factors among which, specifically, a number of institutional factors (mentioned in the previous section).[11] Yet the use of the awkward adjective 'natural' and the slow pace at which institutional changes occur induced many of those who were quick to endorse Phelps' and Friedman's ideas to assume the existence of a constant NRU (see, for example, Barro, 1977 and 1978). In part this can also be explained bearing in mind that little attention was given to the determinants of the natural rate of unemployment.

However, the very idea of a constant NRU was disproved by the actual course of events. As is well known, in the 1970s and 1980s the unemployment rate kept rising steadily in numerous countries for long periods of time without any re-equilibrating trends being noted.

In order to establish a link between theory and reality, as early as 1976 Sargent argued that the strong and persistent fluctuations in the natural rate of unemployment that were registered in subsequent years lead us to assume that any historically recorded rises in unemployment may well stem from structural changes which resulted in a fairly higher equilibrium unemployment level (see Sargent, 1976). This 'structuralistic' view, which traces the natural rate of employment back to a wide spectrum of possible causes, including variously distorted supply mechanisms, high wage rates demanded by unions as well as government intervention into the economy, may well be tautological since any persistent rise in the number of jobless may well be interpreted as evidence that the natural rate of unemployment has increased. Be that as it may, experience has shown that the NRU was far from constant either in the 1970s or in the 1980s.

With reference to the German case, for instance, a 1984 study reported a rise in the natural rate of unemployment from 1.3% at the close of the 1960s to 6.2% in 1981–83 (see Basevi, Blanchard, Buiter, Dornbusch and Layard, 1984) and a further survey carried out in the following year reported a rise in the natural rate from 0.9 to 8% (see Coe and Gagliardi, 1985). As for Great Britain, data evidence so far made available points to an (average) 4% rate between 1970 and 1975 and, conversely, a 10-11% rate between 1981 and 1988. In still another study Layard and Nickell argued that the rate of unemployment at which inflation was stable rose from 2% in the 1950s to 11% in the 1980s (see Layard and Nickell, 1985). Similarly, in France unemployment was (on average) 3% between 1970 and 1975, but ranged between 9 and 10% in the period 1981–88.[12] However, it must be remembered that in the 1990s unemployment rose considerably in most countries with the relevant exception of United States.

In the opinion of many authors, rises in unemployment may stem in part from increased social security expenditure and aid policies in favour of lower-income classes and in part from growing union power. These authors also suggest a third possible cause, namely changes in the housing market, which sizeably reduced the geographical mobility of the labour force (see Healey, 1988, pp. 110–11, Bean, 1994, pp. 585–97).

In the following sections we will show that in actual fact rises in the unemployment level stem from the path dependence of the equilibrium rate of unemployment with respect to the effective rate. In the opinion of some, whenever the effective rate of unemployment is on the increase, the equilibrium unemployment rate also tends to rise and, following a period characterized by a high unemployment level the effective rate of unemployment, far from reverting to its initial value, tends to remain at higher levels.

Other reasons why rates of unemployment rose in particular from 1975 onward can be inferred from a close observation of the actual course of events. In many countries the mobility of the labour force was hampered by the enforcement of numerous restrictions: dismissals became difficult as a consequence of legal bans, wage rates were rigidly blocked at high levels as a result of their automatic adjustment to the cost of living, and unemployment allowances were increased. But the idea that any persistent rise in unemployment must necessarily stem from a rise in the natural rate of unemployment has been the object of fierce criticism. In Europe, the jobless increased from 2% in the 1960s to 10% at the close of the 1980s and approx. 12% in 1996; but no convincing explanation was offered as to the reasons why the natural rate of unemployment should have increased to such an extent. In a 1988 volume edited by Lawrence and Schultze numerous authors discussed empirical evidence in support of the existence of structural factors of various kinds which could be assumed to have driven up the rate of unemployment, reaching the conclusion that the thesis propounded by monetarists old and new alike lacked any solid foundation (see Lawrence and Schultze, 1988). Gordon also reached comparable conclusions in a study published in 1988.

Focusing on the British case, for instance, we may argue that the economic policies enforced by the Thatcher government resulted in a highly different approach which may have caused structural changes in the natural rate of unemployment, but it is highly likely that a distinctively liberalist political approach such as Mrs Thatcher's ought rather to have *reduced*, not driven up, the natural rate of unemployment. How are we consequently to explain the fact that more man-years of work were lost between 1979 and 1987 than over the previous forty-year period? (see Blanchard and Summers, 1988, p. 183 and Jenkinson, 1987, p. 22).

No convincing explanations of the rise in the natural rate of unemployment seem to be at hand at least for the specific case of Britain. There unemployment stood at 5% when the earliest restrictive policies were enforced in 1979 and, instead of diminishing, kept rising steadily to an average of over 11% in the five-year period 1983–1988; thereafter it declined at a very slow pace. Bearing in mind that Mrs Thatcher launched the most daringly liberalistic economic policy experiment ever attempted in any industrial country over the past fifty years, the persistence of such a high unemployment rate over so long a period can barely be explained in the light of the theory of the natural rate of unemployment. In subsequent years the rate of unemployment fell noticeably, but this can in no way account for the situation throughout Mrs Thatcher's long tenure of power.

Probably it is the reflections we have been developing so far that induced Hahn to argue some years ago: 'for my part, I have strong theoretical doubts concerning the concept of a "natural" rate of unemployment' (see Hahn, 1993, p. 9). And we cannot but wholeheartedly subscribe to his opinion.

6.4 HYSTERESIS THEORY AND THE PHILLIPS CURVE

To a large extent the current re-evaluation of Keynesian approaches to economic policy examined in the last part of the previous section is owed to the theory of the *path dependence of the natural rate of unemployment*, according to which the equilibrium rate is determined by the rates of unemployment recorded in the years immediately before, and which is now termed the hysteresis theory.[13] Such an assumption involves denying the theoretical validity of the view that there is a single unemployment rate toward which the system tends.[14] The hysteresis theory is often traced back to Blanchard and Summers (1986, 1987 and 1988),[15] but the appearance of a large number of studies on the subject in the past decade makes it impossible, as of today, to continue associating this theory with any single author or to attribute the path dependence of the NRU (or NAIRU) to a single cause. In point of fact, there are at least three main theoretical explanations of path dependence:[16]

1. the unsolidaristic attitude of insiders;
2. the scant role of long-term unemployment in collective bargaining;
3. capital scrapping.

6.4.1 The unsolidaristic attitude of insiders[17]

The idea that the path dependence of the natural rate is the result of an unsolidaristic attitude on the part of insiders was first suggested by Blanchard and Fischer and can be illustrated using their model as a basis.[18]

Let us write the relevant quantitative theory of money equation using the rates of change of the variables involved:

$$\dot{x}_t = \dot{m}_t - \dot{p}_t \tag{6.1}$$

where $\dot{x}$ is, as usual, the rate of change in income, $\dot{p}$ is the inflation rate and $\dot{m}$ the rate of change in money supply. No term reflecting the velocity of circulation of money appears in the equation since this is assumed to be constant.[19] If returns to scale are constant, the rate of growth in employment ($\dot{n}$) will be:

$$\dot{n}_t = \dot{x}_t - \dot{\pi}_t \tag{6.2}$$

where $\dot{\pi}$ is the rate of growth in labour productivity.

If

$$\dot{p}_t = \dot{w}_t - \dot{\pi}_t \tag{6.3}$$

the result will be:

$$\dot{n}_t = \dot{m}_t - \dot{w}_t \tag{6.4}$$

To solve equation (6.4) we must introduce assumptions concerning the way wages are determined and the growth rate of the quantity of money. The central assumption of Blanchard and Summers is that the rate of growth in money wages is fixed at that level at which *insiders* who are in employment can expect to keep their jobs and firms are not encouraged to hire fresh workers, so that the wages of whose already employed are maximized. Based on (6.4) and assuming the rate of unemployment to be stable when $\dot{n} = 0$,[20] this means that the equation for the growth rate in wages can be written as follows:

$$\dot{w}_t = \dot{m}_t^e \tag{6.5}$$

where the apex reflects the expected value of $\dot{m}$.

At this point let us assume that money supply undergoes unexpected changes and let us write:

$$\dot{m}_t = \dot{m}_t^* + \varepsilon_t \tag{6.6}$$

where ε_t, namely an exogenous shock, has its usual properties (its average value is 0 and variance is constant).

Substituting (6.4) and (6.5) into (6.6), we obtain:

$$\dot{n}_t = \varepsilon_t \qquad (6.7)$$

where $\dot{n}$ is the equilibrium value of the growth rate of employment. From (6.7) we infer that the rate of change in employment (and therefore the natural rate of unemployment) is a random walk with no constant value.

If insiders manage to have money wages increase at the same rate as expected money wages so that the expected employment level remains constant – Blanchard and Summers (1987, p. 291) conclude – the implications of this conduct 'are drastic: employment follows a random walk, with the innovation being due to unexpected movements in aggregate demand'. As the labour force is given, the equilibrium level of employment is equal to the actual employment figure recorded over the period immediately before and the economic system, regardless of recent events, will not tend to return to any given equilibrium value. And

> the mechanism behind this result is transparent: after an adverse shock which reduces employment, workers who are still employed have no desire to cut the nominal wage so as to increase employment (Blanchard and Summers, 1987, p. 291)

the opposite is true when employment increases. As is apparent, the persistence of unemployment and the hysteresis mechanism must be traced back to the unsolidaristic attitude of insiders since by refusing to accept lower wages they keep up the equilibrium rate of unemployment after an adverse shock.

It goes without saying that the above explanation of hysteresis is based on the neoclassical, rather than Keynesian, idea that high wages (and unions which defend them) are the cause of unemployment. Two assumptions are clearly recognized behind Blanchard and Summers' arguments: the unions' only concern is to protect insiders; labour demand is derived from the traditional neoclassical function of production. On the former point we want to object that the idea of unions entirely unconcerned with the problems of the jobless is barely in keeping with historical records in many European countries where they have striven, for better or for worse, to reconcile the interests of those in employment with interests of a more general nature.[21] As for the decreasing relationship between wages and employment which determines that unemployment is caused by high wages, Keynesians, Kaleckians and neo-Marxists are known to accept

Sraffa's well-known criticism of the neoclassical theory of production or, in any case, to hold the view that 'there is no dogmatic position on the consequences for employment of higher real wages' (Riach, 1995, p. 173).[22]

6.4.2   The scant role of long-term unemployment (in collective bargaining)

The second argument that is often used to explain the path dependence of the equilibrium rate of unemployment is the different weight in collective bargaining of those who have long been out of work as compared to those who have lost their jobs more recently.[23] With the passing of time, it is argued, unemployment deteriorates human resources both because workers not involved in the production process no longer receive any training and may even lose their former working skills and also because they become less 'presentable', as it were (see Blanchard, Diamond, 1990, pp. 10–12). Furthermore, with the passing of time their job search becomes progressively less intense (Layard, Nickell, 1986, 1987) and this is one more reason why the weight of the long-term jobless in collective bargaining is bound to decrease.

The action of only one of these factors is enough to reduce the number of jobless competing for a job at a given wage rate and will consequently drive up the equilibrium wage rate.

It is clear that to a certain extent the explanation of hysteresis in terms of long-term unemployment recalls the argument set forth in the previous paragraph, in particular because it draws a distinction between two categories of workers (definable as insiders and outsiders in this case also) based on their respective involvement in the production process. However, this explanation of hysteresis is more in line with the non-neoclassical tradition of political economy because it emphasizes, not an unsolidaristic attitude on the part of unions, but subjective and institutional mechanisms which result in perverse – and irreversible – 'cumulative' relations between unemployment and the deterioration of human resources. As for the former (the subjective factors), we are thinking of the loss in terms of specific and general working skills.[24] In the opinion of Sawyer:

> Unemployment will not only affect those directly experiencing it, but persistent unemployment will influence general culture. The work ethic is unlikely to have much appeal to those who cannot find work, and who can see that their neighbours also cannot find work. When employment is not available people have to find other activities to fill their time, with the development of alternative non-working cultures. These other activities can range from idleness and apathy through drug dependence

and crime. A return to full employment will, in effect, have to reverse the path dependence of prolonged unemployment: for example work ethic may have been lost in many communities and would have to be gradually restored (Sawyer, 1995, pp. 24–5).

Another subjective factor is the mistrust with which employers look upon those who have remained out of work for a fairly long period of time. Among objective factors, in addition to declining job search intensity on the part of the long-term jobless, let us mention the role of institutions which guarantee the jobless an income of some sort (in manners and for periods of time varying from country to country), fresh work opportunities or access to vocational training schemes, although the long-run jobless are usually not eligible for such benefits.

A graph which is often used to represent the path dependence of the NRU (or NAIRU) caused by changes in the number of the long-term jobless has been reproduced in Figure 6.1.[25] *PRW* reflects the real wage offered by firms, which is assumed to be unrelated to employment and thus to remain fixed at $0A$; conversely, *BRW* reflects the increasing relationship between the real wage demanded by workers and the employment level. *BRW* is plotted for a given value of long-term unemployment and will consequently be shifted to the left every time long-term unemployment increases: each fresh employment level is matched by greater wage pressure, since the number of jobless who are more likely to find fresh jobs and play an active role in bargaining has shrunk.

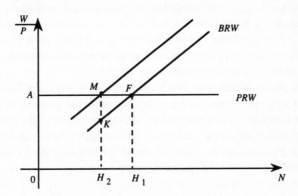

Figure 6.1   The effect of long-run unemployment

At this point let us assume that the starting situation is F, which is the NAIRU of our model because the real wage rate demanded at the employment level $0H_1$ equals the rate offered. Let us also assume that F is not associated with any changes in long-term unemployment. If a demand shock drives down employment to the level at $0H_2$, in the short run the system will tend to move towards K; but if, subsequently, unemployment persists and generates a rise in the number of long-term jobless, for the reasons mentioned above BRW will be shifted to the left and the interception with PRW will be, for example, M, which means that the NAIRU has increased.[26]

6.4.3 Capital scrapping

As shown by Bean (1994, p. 612), some authors have traced the path dependence of the natural rate of unemployment back to 'shortage of capital'. A particular model proposed in this connection is Carlin and Soskice's (1989), which ascribes the path dependence of the NAIRU to the mechanism of capital scrapping. In periods of rising unemployment, when unemployment exceeds the natural rate, employers are little inclined to provide for the proper maintenance of their capital goods or, in slightly different words, in situations of rising unemployment and, thus, low capital utilization, their machinery is left 'to rust'; this, by reducing production capacity, pushes up the equilibrium rate of unemployment (which is specifically associated with the utilization rate of capital goods).

As things stand, this argument of Carlin and Soskice's follows the same lines as the one presented for labour in the previous paragraph: just as workers lose their work skills, so too will capital goods lose their production potential when they are not used. But the process discussed by Carlin and Soskice does not substantially differ from the idea of 'capital decumulation' in periods of crisis (Bean, 1994) or from Rowthorn's idea of an inverse relationship between unemployment and accumulation (decumulation) of capital (Rowthorn 1995 and 1996).[27]

In all these cases the underlying rationale is as follows: firms deem it convenient to leave a certain part of their production capacity unused and make their investment (and capital goods maintenance) decisions in such a way as to bring the actual degree of utilization of their capital goods in line with a precise target level. When production declines (or fails to increase in proportion to the rise in labour productivity) – and employment and capital goods utilization likewise decrease – firms will respond by undercutting their previous investment decisions (or the extent to which they intended to maintain their capital goods). This will obviously result in a different relation between unemployment and capital utilization in subsequent periods, so that the same unemployment level will be associated with a higher capital utilization rate.

But if the compatibility of the claims of both social parties (workers and capitalists/firms and unions) is associated both with unemployment and with capital utilization, the unemployment–inflation trade-off will worsen in periods of low investment (or insufficient maintenance of capital goods) and it will take a higher rate of unemployment to obtain stable prices (or a constant inflation rate). Conversely, the trade-off will tend to improve in periods of booming economic activity.

A simple graph may be useful in this case too (Figure 6.2). Let v on the ordinate be the capital utilization rate and u on the abscissa the rate of unemployment. As the capital stock is given, there will be an inverse relationship (FP) between the two variables because the capital utilization rate decreases in periods of rising employment. This function will be shifted every time firms make a net investment, whether positive or negative, because any such investment causes a change in the capital stock.

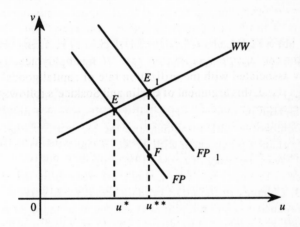

Figure 6.2   Capital scrapping

At this point we will consider the relation which results from all the combinations of u and v at which the wage rate demanded by workers is compatible with the rate offered by firms (WW). The relation is an increasing one because, as firms can be expected to aim at greater profit margins in periods of rising capital utilization rates and workers are assumed to lay in higher wage claims in periods of declining unemployment, the wage rate offered by firms will only equal the rate demanded by workers when increases of u are associated with increases of v as well. At all points along *WW* firms are satisfied with the capital utilization/mark-up combination they have achieved.[28] The two curves meet in E – which corresponds to a NAIRU equal to u^*. Consequently the system will persist in the situation reflected in E as long as aggregate demand generates the unemployment level reflected in u^*.

At this point we will assume that a restrictive economic policy gives rise to a deflationary trend or that an exogenous shock drives down aggregate demand. Initially the system will move to F, unemployment will rise to u^{**} and incomes and employment will begin to decline: the result will be a fall in the capital utilization rate. If firms cut plant maintenance expenditure and/or existing capital goods are left 'to rust', FP will be shifted to the right and will become FP_1: indeed, as part of the capital goods previously used in production have been 'scrapped', each fresh unemployment level will be associated with a higher plant utilization rate. The new equilibrium point will be E_1, at which the unemployment level compatible with price (or inflation) stability has increased to u^{**}.

6.5   IS HYSTERESIS COMPATIBLE WITH THE THEORY OF THE *NATURAL RATE OF UNEMPLOYMENT*?

To represent the rationale behind the hysteresis mechanism and establish to what extent this particular explanation of persistently high unemployment levels is compatible with Friedman and the monetarists' theory of the natural rate of unemployment or with the Keynesians' theory of the NAIRU we can follow in the wake of Cross (1995a, pp. 181–200).

Changes in income caused by a shock are marked on the abscissa of Figure 6.3. Changes in the GDP brought about by positive shocks (for instance expansive economic policies) are found to the right of point 0, while negative changes due to adverse shocks (for instance a restrictive monetary policy) lie to the left of that point. Let us now assume we are setting out from a situation characterized by an unemployment level equal to the natural rate A and by no shocks. The graph in Figure 6.3 shows the path which follows upon a shock according to the theory of the natural rate of unemployment. In the event of an adverse shock, for example, the system will move from point A to point B and will then revert to point A; likewise, in the event of a positive shock it will move from A to C and then revert to A. It goes without saying that A is associated with a value of u which is the only existing equilibrium rate of unemployment.

The graph in Figure 6.4 shows developments registered from the perspective of the hysteresis theory. Again we will assume that the initial situation is point A. When an adverse shock occurs (for instance the enforcement of a restrictive monetary policy) the system will again move to B, i.e. to a higher unemployment rate, but subsequently there will be no return from B to A, but a movement from B to D. In the event of a positive shock (the expansive policy), the shift will not be from C to A, but from C to K – because the processes mentioned before (namely the disqualification (or requalification) of the labour force or capital stock adjustments to lower (or higher) levels will have occurred during the movement from A to B (or C). Thus the graph shows that the theory of the natural rate of unemployment is in stark opposition to path dependence: in Figure 6.4 the properties of point A are in no way different from those of points D and K, which lie on the same line, OM, and there is no single equilibrium rate of unemployment towards which the system tends.[29]

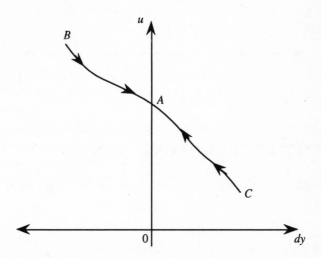

Figure 6.3   The persistency of unemployment

Consequently this reconstruction bears out the differences between the hysteresis theory and the theories of persistent unemployment: while the latter can be assumed to explain the obstacles encountered by the system when reverting from B (or C) to A (Figure 6.3) and can be reconciled with the theory of the natural rate thanks to the assumption that the system will always revert to A in the long term, path dependence is not at all compatible with the hypothesis of a single equilibrium rate of unemployment, either with the NRU of neoclassical tradition or with the NAIRU of the Keynesian models of the 1970s and 1980s because it assumes the existence of multiple equilibria.

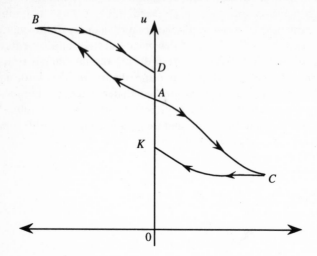

Figure 6.4   The hysteresis of NRU

6.6   HYSTERESIS: TWO CONSEQUENCES

The effects of the introduction of p*ath-dependence* on the equilibrium level of unemployment may be said to be of two main kinds:

A. In theoretical terms, path dependence further *disproves the stability of the Phillips curve*, though in a different way from that traditionally theorized by Lipsey, Friedman and Phelps. As mentioned above in Section 6.4, it becomes absolutely impossible to speak of a single equilibrium level of unemployment either in a short-term view or in the medium-long run, whereas it becomes possible to speak of *multiple equilibria* (see, inter alia, Summers, 1988, pp. 19–25; McDonald, 1995, pp. 101–52).
B. In terms of economic policy, the effect is a re-evaluation of the *demand-management* policy theory which, as said before, seemed to have been definitively disproved by Phelps' and Friedman's criticisms of the Phillips curve. In point of fact, if the hysteresis hypothesis is accepted, the NAIRU may be reduced by growths in aggregate demand capable of improving the trade-off in later years.

With reference to the first point, however, it would be appropriate to develop some further considerations. As mentioned above, Summers has argued that the Phillips curve is definitively confuted by the introduction of the hysteresis hypothesis, i.e. that the famous curve which played such an unprecedented role in the debate on inflation and unemployment is about to be superseded by more appropriate interpretative paradigms. On closer examination, however, this theory can also be viewed from a different perspective and the path-dependence of the equilibrium rate may appear as an attempt to rehabilitate the original Phillips curve.[30]

Let us write this simple model (see Gordon, 1989):

$$\dot{p}_t = \dot{p}_t^e - \beta\left(u_t - u_t^*\right) \qquad (6.8)$$

$$u_t^* = \mu\, u_{t-1} + z_t \qquad (6.9)$$

$$\dot{p}_t^e = \dot{p}_{t-1} \qquad (6.10)$$

where p is the rate of inflation, u the rate of unemployment, u^* the natural unemployment rate, the subscripts t and $t-1$ refer to time, the superscript e reflects expected values and z reflect the microeconomic determinants of the unemployment. To make things easier, in (6.10) we have assumed static inflationary expectations. If, for the sake of simplicity, it is assumed that $\mu = 1$, the Phillips curve will be:

$$\dot{p}_t = \dot{p}_{t-1} - \beta\left(u_t - u_{t-1}\right) + \beta z_t \qquad (6.11)$$

In this case, within an economy with static expectations points such as A and B in Figure 6.5 are all long-term equilibrium points and the NRU equals the actual unemployment rate in the previous period ($u_t^* = u_{t-1}$). Assuming that demand-boosting policies result in shifting the economy to the position at B, the system will tend to remain at B because the inflation trends expected for subsequent periods, $0C$, will be perfectly verified and unemployment will reach its fresh equilibrium level at $0D$.

It goes without saying that both the assumption of 'static' expectations and that of a perfect adjustment of the natural rate of unemployment to the actual rate of the previous period can be changed without substantially changing the results obtained.

Indeed, if forecasts are still made dependent on the past trend of the inflation rate and admitting that the natural rate of unemployment is to some extent dependent on the actual rate, an unemployment/inflation relation of the type suggested by Phillips in 1958 will remain possible even in the event of correct inflation forecasts[31].

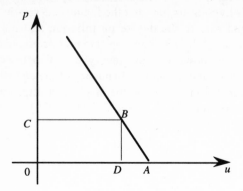

Figure 6.5   The hysteresis of NRU and the Phillips curve

If

$$\dot{p}_t^e = (1-\gamma)\sum_{i=1}^{\infty} \gamma^{i-1}\dot{p}_{t-i} \qquad (6.12)$$

and the required substitutions are made in equation (6.8), the result is that the unemployment rate at which it is possible to make correct inflation forecasts will depend on the actual unemployment rate in the previous period.

In point of fact:

$$\dot{p}_t = (1-\gamma)\sum_{i=1}^{\infty} \gamma^{i-1}\dot{p}_{t-i} \qquad (6.13)$$

implies that:

$$u_{nt} = z_t + \mu u_{t-1} \qquad (6.14)$$

so that the criticisms of the NRU set forth by theoreticians of path dependence lead to a Phillips curve with a large spectrum of possible equilibrium situations. And this new curve, which resembles the original one proposed in 1958, turns yet again into a Keynesian curve with a 'menu' of possible economic policy options. Thus the importance of this new Phillips curve also lies in the fact that it confers fresh dignity on Keynesian demand-management policies as a means of combating unemployment.[32]

With reference to the last observation, i.e. the second point mentioned at the beginning of this section, it is worth underlining that the hysteresis theory can be considered a modern rebuttal of the neoclassical dichotomy between the real and monetary sectors (see Mankiw, 1993, and Dixon, 1995).

As is well known, all neoclassical economists have invariably been supporters of the quantitative theory of money and still hold steadfastly to the idea of a straightforward dichotomy between the real and monetary sectors by assuming changes in the latter to have no bearing on real variables. This means that they share the views of many classical theorists, above all Hume, which were later formalized and expounded in detail in a famous book by Patinkin published in 1965. As mentioned above (fn. 2), this text is a fundamental point of reference for the theory of the natural rate of unemployment considered as a new designation for the concept of full employment.

The reflections developed in the previous pages clearly indicate that in a Keynesian approach to macroeconomics one of the merits of the hysteresis theory is its criticism of the classical dichotomy: as shown by Figure 6.4 in Section 4, shocks following changes in monetary magnitudes (e.g. changes in money supply) can have short and long term effects on the equilibrium value of real magnitudes (income level, unemployment rate, etc.) (see Dixon, 1995, pp. 57–74) and Keynesian policies, whether real or monetary, can thus produce real effects.

6.7 CONCLUSION

In macroeconomic debates confrontations between different schools often proceed along a path which depends on the theories then in vogue, on actual economic trends in progress or the genius of a particular economist who manages to focus the attention of academics on new ways of addressing new or age-old problems. There is no denying that the history of the interpretations of the Phillips curve is a concrete example of the great vitality of the debate between schools.

In due time the quarrel over different interpretations of this celebrated curve focused on the point where the curve intercepts the abscissa. Two different but interdependent questions take on greater significance in this respect: the 'optimality' of the NRU/NAIRU and the problem of the role played by demand-management policies with respect to medium or long term equilibria. Over the last few decades the stances of different schools of thought on these points have been varying from agreement to stark dissent, giving rise to two distinct phases in the debate between Keynesians and monetarists (new classical) on the Phillips curve and economic policy.

The first phase was mainly marked by the opposition between NRU theorists and NAIRU theorists, a distinction which had nothing to do with the second point. Subscribing to the monetarist theses concerning the verticality of the Phillips curve in the long run, the NAIRU theorists admitted that demand-management policies would not be effective in the long run even in the presence of substantial involuntary unemployment. Fiscal and monetary policies would play a marginal role and, moreover, this role would be confined to cases in which exogenous shocks were found to push up the rate of unemployment well beyond the natural rate.

Until the late 1980s the theses of these two schools diverged exclusively on the nature of the equilibrium rate of unemployment. According to the NRU theorists unemployment was not in itself a problem which economic policy was supposed to tackle if not with the intention to restore flexibility in the labour market. Blinder has quite rightly noted that the theory of the NRU inherently implies the idea that economic policy makers must 'accept high unemployment with resignation, as a phenomenon generated by nature' (see Blinder, 1989, p. 2). Conversely, from the perspective of NAIRU theorists the equilibrium rate of unemployment was in no way an optimal situation and it needed fresh economic policy strategies alternative to aggregate demand boosting policies in order to lower the NAIRU: the involuntary unemployment implied in the NAIRU was doubtlessly to be contrasted, but with incomes policies or structural measures.

In the second phase the divergences concerning the first point gradually petered out: while everyone, even monetarists, acknowledged the importance to be attached to 'structural' policies in lowering the equilibrium rate of unemployment, a conflict arise over the kind of *structural policies* that were to be prioritized as well as the part demand-management policies were to play. Ever since the acceptance of the path dependence of the NRU (or NAIRU), most advocates of non-neoclassical approaches to macroeconomics have criticized the dichotomy between the real and monetary sectors with fresh courage and, reappraising the Phillips curve and Keynesian ideas on aggregate demand policies, have emphasized that fiscal and monetary policies play a much more significant role than merely helping the economy converge toward the equilibrium rate of unemployment.

NOTES

1. In this chapter we intend to use the word 'Keynesian' in a fairly wide sense, i.e. to class as Keynesians many economists who adopt models other than the demand and supply model of the neoclassical tradition.
2. Dixon, 1995, pp. 57–65, argues that the NRU is associated with the notion of full employment proposed in Patinkin, 1965. The equation of the NRU with full employment was dealt with extensively in the literature of the 1980s, but further references to it are found, for example, in the 1994 edition of Dornbusch and Fischer's popular book: see Dornbusch and Fischer, 1994, pp. 208 and 505–6.
3. That is why it is certainly right to say that 'the severest blow on Keynesianism in the 50's and 60's was the advent of the idea of the natural rate of unemployment' (see Jackman, Layard and Pissarides, 1986, p. 111).
4. From among those who equated the NRU with the NAIRU, see Blanchard and Fischer, 1989, pp. 543–4, and Hall and Taylor, 1988, p. 131. See, also, Layard and Nickell, 1985; Johnson and Layard, 1986.
5. The concept of NIRU (Not Inflationary Rate of Unemployment) was first theorized by Modigliani and Papademus (1975), while Rowthorn (1977) was probably the first to suggest the existence of a NAIRU without using this particular acronym. For a criticism of the designation NAIRU, see Cross, 1995a, p. 184.
6. For an analysis of this type of Phillips curve in the first period see, inter alia, Samuelson and Solow, 1960; Bowen and Berry, 1963; Kaliski, 1964; Gylfason and Lindbeck, 1982.
7. From among those who insist on the clear-cut distinction between NRU and NAIRU let us mention, in particular, Cornwall, 1983, pp. 66–9 and 1989, pp. 99–100; 1994, pp.44–64; Tobin, 1995, pp. 37–9. For a different distinction between NRU and NAIRU, see Clark and Laxaton, 1997, pp. 15–17.
8. In a letter to Rod Cross dated November 2nd, 1990 (quoted on p. 1 of Cross's Introduction to Cross (ed.), 1995b), Friedman states that: 'the crucial element is that nominal magnitudes must be sharply distinguished from real magnitudes, and that nominal magnitudes in and of themselves cannot determine real magnitudes'. Cross continues 'Thus the NRH postulates the autonomy of the structural characteristics of labour and commodities markets and applies the doctrine of monetary neutralities to unemployment'.
9. This is why so many heterodox authors in the 1980s rejected the Phillips curve straightaway (see Palley, 1996, pp. 166–81).

10. See, for example, Summers, 1986, Krashewski, 1988; for a survey, see, also, Bean 1994. A somewhat different approach has been proposed in a recent essay by Leeson who suggests that deflationary policies end up by being caught in an *expectations trap* when unemployment rises excessively and the Phillips curve becomes horizontal. See Leeson, 1997.

11. In this connection it is worth mentioning that Friedman himself stressed right from the start that "the natural rate of unemployment [is not] immutable. On the contrary, many aspects of the market which determine its level are the product of human action and stem from precise political choices" (see Friedman, 1968, p. 9).

12. For a review of the evolution of *facts* and *theories* until the early 1990s, see Bean, 1994.

13. Some authors distinguish between hysteresis and persistent unemployment (see below, Section 6.5).

14. According to a widely accepted formulation, hysteresis sets in when, at the end of a temporary fluctuation in an economic system, the values of the variables do not return to their levels before the change (see, *inter alia*, Cross and Hutchinson, 1988, p. 3; for a more detailed definition, see Wyplosz, 1987, p. 124; Katzner, 1993, and Setterfield, 1993). See also Cross, 1995a, pp. 181–200, where the differences between hysteresis and persistence are dealt with.

15. From among the earliest references to hysteresis phenomena, see that contained in Phelps, 1972; see also Phelps, 1995, Salop, 1979 and Heagraves Heap, 1980. For a brief history of the concept, see Franz, 1990.

16. Some models trace path-dependence back to other aspects, such as technological and organisational innovation intensity (Blinder, 1988) or changes in union competitiveness (Skott, 1989). Fairly similar classifications are proposed in Franz, 1990, pp. 8–13, Bean, 1994, pp. 603–14 and Jones, 1995, pp. 8–9 and 15–36. For a different view of hysteresis, see Cottrel, 1984–5. See also Neville, 1979.

17. See Blanchard and Summers, 1986, 1987, 1988.

18. In actual fact this is a simplification of the model proposed in Blanchard, Summers, 1987.

19. Irrespective of the process according to which money supply is held to be created, the assumption of a constant velocity of circulation of money is not in line with the Keynesian tradition.

20. This is just another simplifying hypothesis in the absence of which the results would not substantially change.

21. This is the type of union Tarantelli used to term 'reformist'; see Tarantelli, 1986, pp. 10–21.

22. In Screpanti 1996 (especially pp. 93–5), the assumption that the behaviour of those employed is the cause of hysteresis in the NRU is explained in a different manner which is more in keeping with the Kaleckian and neo-Marxist traditions of political economy.

23. This argument was initially proposed in Phelps, 1972 and Hargreaves Heap, 1980, p. 615. More recently it was developed in Layard and Nickell, 1987; Blanchard and Diamond, 1990. Two different versions are suggested in Archibald, 1995, pp. 99–100 and Sawyer, 1995, pp. 24–5.

24. For a review of social psychology contributions dealing with the effects of unemployment on human resources, see Darity, Goldsmith, 1993, and for a different approach to these issues, see Archibald, 1995.

25. See Carlin and Soskice, 1990, pp. 452–6. A different graph is proposed in Blanchard, 1997, pp. 308–10.

26. Carlin and Soskice, 1990, p. 455, throw light on a mechanism whereby the change in the NAIRU would appear as a short-term phenomenon instead of a long-term one. In this way they seem to reconcile hysteresis with the NAIRU. As far as we are concerned here, the graph in Figure 6.1 is only intended to provide an initial picture of the phenomena described in this paragraph and seems to be compatible with the path dependence of the long-term NAIRU.

27. On the relations between unemployment and capital accumulation, see also Rowthorn, 1996.

28. Carlin and Soskice, 1989, also introduce a straight line, v^*v^*, parallel to the abscissa, to suggest that firms tend to a given constant degree of capital utilization, but this does not seem to fit in with the notion of *WW* as a geometrical locus of the points at which firms are satisfied with their situations (and this must necessarily hold both with respect to the mark-up and the degree of utilization).

29. Obviously the system can also have a set of possible equilibrium points which is smaller than the whole *OM* segment. See Cross, 1995a, p. 193.

30. For a different rebuttal of Summers's criticism of the Phillips curve, see Clark and Laxaton, 1997, who set out to rehabilitate the (non-linear) Phillips curve and show how a stabilization policy drives down the NAIRU as a consequence of the non-linear shape of the curve and the asymmetric response (in the way suggested by Tobin) of wages to unemployment.

31. A different opinion is expounded in Lesson, 1994.

32. Bruno, 1988, contains a criticism of writings from the 1980s which claimed to be Keynesian, but whose disregard of global demand control policies actually conflicted with Keynesian stances.

Bibliography

Akerlof, G.A., Dickens, W.T. and Perry, G.L.(1996), 'The Macroeconomics of Low inflation', *Brookings Papers on Economic Activity*, no. 1, pp. 1–59.

Alchian, A.A. (1970), 'Information Costs Pricing and Resource Unemployment', in Phelps (1970b), pp. 27–52.

Alchian, A.A. and Demsetz, N. (1972), 'Production, Information Costs and Economic Organization', *American Economic Review*, vol. 62, no. 5, December, pp. 777–95.

Amendola, A. (ed.) (1995), *Disoccupazione. Analisi macroeconomica e mercato del lavoro*, ESI, Napoli.

Ando, A. and Brayton, F. (1995), 'Prices, Wages and Employment in the US Economy: A Traditional Model and Tests of Some Alternative', in Cross (ed.) (1995b), pp. 256–98.

Arcelli, M. (ed.) (1992), *Il ruolo della banca centrale nella politica economica*, Il Mulino, Bologna.

Archibald, G.G. (1969), 'The Phillips Curve and the Distribution of Unemployment', *American Economic Review*, vol. 59, no. 2, May, pp. 124–34.

Archibald, G.C. (1995), 'Hysteresis and Memory in the Labour Market, in Cross (ed.) (1995), pp. 90–100.

Arestis P. and Marshall M. (eds) (1995), *The Political Economy of Full Employment*, Edward Elgar Ltd., Aldershot.

Argy, V. (1981), *The Postwar International Money Crisis; an Analysis*, London.

Ashenfelter, O. (ed.) (1986), *Handbook of Labour Economy*, Vol II, North Holland, Amsterdam.

Asimakopulos, A. (1975), 'A Kaleckian Theory of Income Distribution', *Canadian Journal of Economics*, vol. 8, no. 3, August, pp. 313–333.

Asimakopulos, A., (1980–81), 'Theme in a Post-Keynesian Theory of Income Distribution', *Journal of Post Keynesian Economics*, vol. 3, no. 2, Winter, pp. 158–69.

Ball, L., Mankiw, N.G. and Romer, D. (1988), 'The New Keynesian Economics and the Output-Inflation Trade-Off', *Brookings Papers on Economic Activity*, no. 1, pp. 1–82.

Barrel R. (ed.) (1994), *The U.K. Labour Market*, Cambridge University Press, Cambridge.

Barro, R. (1977), 'Unanticipated Money Growth and Unemployment in the United State', *American Economic Review*, no. 67, March, pp. 101–15.

Barro, R. (1978), 'Unanticipated Money, Output and the Price Level in the United States, *Journal of Political Economy*, vol. 86, no. 4, August, pp. 549–80.

Barron, J.M., Bisho, J. and Dunkelberg, W.C. (1985), 'Employer Search: the Interviewing and Hiring of New Employees', *Review of Economics and Statistics*, vol. 67, no. 1, February, pp. 43–52.

Basevi, G., Blanchard, O.J., Buiter, W.H., Dornbush, R. and Layard, R. (1984), 'Europe: The Case for Unsustainable Growth', *CEPS Paper*, no. 8–9, Bruxelles.

Basile, L. and Salvadori, N. (1984–85), 'Kalecki's Pricing Theory', *Journal of Post Keynesian Economics*, vol. 7, no. 2, Winter, pp. 249–62.

Bathia, R.J. (1962), 'Profits and the Rate of Change in Money Earnings in the United States, 1900–58, *Economica*, vol. 29, no. 115, August, pp. 255–62.

Baumol, W.J. (1952), *Welfare Economics and the Theory of the State*, Longanous, London.

Bean, C.R. (1992a), 'Identifying the Causes of British Unemployment', London School of Economics, Centre for Economic Performance, Seminar Paper, 23 October.

Bean, C.R. (1992b), 'European Unemployment: A Survey', London School of Economics, Centre for Economic Performance, Discussion Paper 71.

Bean, C.R. (1994), 'European Unemployment', *Journal of Economic Literature*, vol. 32, no. 2, June, pp. 573–619.

Bean, C.R., Layard, R. and Nickell, S., (1986), *The Rise in Unemployment*, Basil Blackwell, Oxford.

Bergstrom, A.R. *et al.* (1978), *Stability and Inflation*, Wiley & Sons Ltd., Chichester.

Blanchard, O.J. (1997), *Macroeconomics*, Prentice-Hall, Upper Saddle River, New Jersey.

Blanchard, O.J. and Fischer, S. (1989), *Lectures in Macroeconomics*, The MIT Press, Cambridge, Mass.

Blanchard, O.J. and Summers, L.H. (1986), 'Hysteresis and the European Unemployment Problem', *NBER Macroeconomics Annual*, Cambridge, Mass.

Blanchard, O.J. and Summers, L.H. (1987), 'Hysteresis in Unemployment', *European Economic Review*, no. 31, February-March, pp. 288–295.

Blanchard, O.J. and Summers, L.H. (1988), 'Beyond The Natural Rate Hypothesis', *American Economic Review*, vol. 78, no. 2, May, pp. 182–193.

Blanchard, O.J. and Diamond, P. (1990), 'Unemployment and Wages', Lecture Prepared for the Employment Institute, London, Mimeo.

Blinder, A.S. (1988), 'The Challenge of High Employment', in Blinder (1989), pp. 139–59.

Blinder, A.S. (1989), *Macroeconomics Under Debate*, Harvester Wheatsheaf, New York.

Borjas, G.J. (1996), *Labor Economics*, McGraw-Hill, New York.

Bowen, W.G. and Berry, R.A. (1963), 'Unemployment Conditions and Movements of the Money Wage Level', in *Review of Economics and Statistics*, vol. 45, no. 2, May, pp. 163–72.

Brunetta, R. and Carraro, C. (1992), 'Le politiche dei redditi come strategie cooperative', in Scandizzo (ed.) (1992).

Brunner, K., Cukierman, K. and Meltzer, A.H. (1980), 'Stagflation, Persistent Unemployment and the Permanence of Economic Shocks', *Journal of Monetary Economics*, vol. 6, pp. 467–92.

Bruno, S., (1988), 'The Secret Story of the Rediscovery of Classical Unemployment and Its Consequences on Economic Advisers', *Studi Economici*, vol. 43, no. 36, pp. 3–37.

Butkiewicz, J.L., Koford, K.J. and Miller, J.B. (eds) (1986), *Keynes' Economic Legacy: Contemporary Economic Theory*, Praeger, New York.

Calmfors, L. and Driffil, J. (1988), 'Bargaining Structure, Corporatism and Macroeconomic Performance', *Economic Policy*, no. 6, April, pp. 13–47.

Carlin, W. and Soskice, D. (1989), 'Medium-Run Keynesianism: Hysteresis and Capital Scrapping', in Davidson and Kregel (1989), pp. 241–255.

Carlin, W. and Soskice, D. (1990), *Macroeconomics and Wage Bargaining*, Oxford University Press, Oxford.

Casavola, P. and Sestito, P. (1995), 'Come si cerca e come si ottiene un lavoro? Un quadro sintetico sull'Italia e alcune implicazioni macroeconomiche', in Amendola (ed.) (1995), pp. 391–430.

CEPR (1995), European Unemployment: Is there a Solution?, Centre for Economic Policy Research, London.

Chrïstal, K.A. and Price S. (1994), *Controversies in Macroeconomics*, Harvester Wheatsheaf, London.

Clark, K.B. and Summers, L.H. (1979), 'Labor Market Dynamics and Unemployment: a Reconsideration', *Brookings Papers on Economic Activity*, no. 1, pp. 13–61.

Clark, P. and Laxaton, D. (1997), 'Phillips Curve, Phillips Lines and the Unemployment Costs of Overheating', *LSE Discussion Paper*, no. 344, April.

Clower, R.W. (1965), 'The Keynesian Counter-Revolution: a Theoretical Appraisal', in Hahn and Brechling (eds) (1965), pp. 103–25.

Coe, D. and Gagliardi, P. (1985), *Nominal Wage Determination in Ten OECD Economies*, OECD, Paris.

Colander, D.C. (ed.) (1979), *Solutions to Inflation*, Harcourt Brace, Javanovich, New York.

Colander, D.C. (1992), 'A Real Theory of Inflation and Incentive Anti-Inflation Plan', *American Economic Review*, vol. 82, no. 2, May, pp. 335–45.

Cornwall, J. (1983), *The Conditions for Economic Recovery*, Blackwell, Oxford.

Corwall, J. (1994), *Economic Breakdown and Recovery: Theory and Policy*, M.E Sharpe, New York.

Corwall, J. and Cornwall, W. (1997), 'The Unemployment Problem and the Legacy of Keynes', *Journal of Post Keynesian Economics*, vol. 19, no. 4, Summer, pp. 525–42.

Corry, B. and Laidler D. (1967), 'The Phillips Relation: a Theoretical Explanation', *Economica*, vol. 34, no. 134, May, pp. 189–97.

Corry, B. and Laidler, D. (1968), 'The Phillips Relation: a Theoretical Explanation. A Reply', *Economica*, vol. 35, no. 138, May, p. 184.

Cottrel, A. (1984-85), 'Keynesianism and the Natural Rate of Unemployment: a Problem of Pedagogy', *Journal of Post Keynesian Economics*, vol. 8, no. 2, pp. 263–8.

Coutts, K., Tarling, R. and Wilkinson, F. (1976), 'Wage Bargaining and the Inflation Process', *Cambridge Economic Policy Review*, vol. 2, no. 1, March, pp. 20–27.

Cripps, F. (1977), 'Money Supply, Wages and Inflation', *Cambridge Journal of Economics*, vol. 1, no. 1, March, pp. 101–112.

Cripps, F. and Godley, W.A. (1976), 'A Formal Analysis of the Cambridge Economic Policy Group Model', *Economica*, vol. 43, no. 172, November, pp. 335–48.

Cross, R. (ed.) (1988), *Unemployment, Hysteresis and the Natural Rate Hypothesis*, Basil Blackwell, Oxford.

Cross, R. (ed.) (1995a), 'Is the Natural Rate Hypothesis Consistent with Hysteresis?', in Cross (ed.) (1995b), pp. 181–200.

Cross, R. (ed.) (1995b), *The Natural Rate of Unemployment*, Cambridge University Press, Cambridge.

Cross, R. and Hutchinson, H. (1988), 'Hysteresis Effects and Unemployment: on Outline', in Cross (ed.) (1988), pp. 3–7.

Darity, W.J. and Goldsmith, A.H. (1993), 'Unemployment, Social Psycology and Unemployment Hysteresis', *Journal of Post Keynesian Economics*, vol. 16, no. 1, Fall, pp. 55–71.

Davidson, P. (1967), 'A Keynesian View of Patinkin's Theory of Employment', *Economic Journal*, vol. 77, no. 307, September, pp. 559–78.

Davidson, P. (1983), 'The Dubious Labor Market Analysis in Meltzer's Restatement', in *Journal of Economic Literature*, vol. 21, no. 1, March, pp. 52–56.

Davidson, P. and Smolensky, E. (1964), *Aggregate Supply and Demand Analysis*, Harper & Row, New York.

Desai, M. (1981), *Testing Monetarism*, Frances Pinter, London.

Destefanis, S. (1991), *The Macroeconomic Analysis of Wage-Indexation. A Case Study for Italy*, PhD Thesis, Cambridge.

Devine, P. (1974), 'Inflation and Marxist Theory', *Marxism Today*, March, pp. 79–92.

Dicks-Mireaux, L.A. and Dow, J.C.R. (1959), 'The Determinants of Wage Inflation: United Kingdom, 1946–56', *Journal of Royal Statistical Society'*, no. 122, Series A , Part II, pp. 145–74.

Dixon, H. (1995), 'Of Coconuts, Decomposition and a Jackass: the Genealogy of the Natural Rate', in Cross (ed.) (1995), pp. 57–74.

Dornbusch, R. and Layard, R. (eds) (1987), *The Performance of the British Economy*, Clarendon Press, Oxford.

Dornbusch, R. and Fischer, S. (1994), *Macroeconomics*, McGraw-Hill, New York.

Downs, A. (1957), *An Economic Theory of Democracy*, New York.

Eatwell, J., Milgate, M. and Newman, P. (eds) (1987), *The New Palgrave. Dictionary of Economics*, Macmillan, London.

Eckstein, O. and Brinner, R. (1972), *The Inflation Process in the United States: A Study Prepared for the Joint Economic Committee*, U.S. Congress, U.S. Government Printing Office, Washington, February.

Elliot, R. (1991), *Labour Economics: a Comparative Text*, McGraw-Hill, London.

Fallick, J.L. and Elliot, R.F. (1981), *Incomes Policies, Inflation and Relative Pay*, Allen & Unwin, London.

Fisher, D. (1988), *Monetary and Fiscal Policy*, Macmillan, London.

Fisher, I. (1926), 'A Statistical Relation between Unemployment and Price Changes', *International Labour Review*, June, pp. 785–92; reprinted in *Journal of Political Economy*, March-April 1973, pp. 495–502.

Fitoussi, J.P. (ed.) (1995), *Economics in a Changing World*, St. Martin Press, New York.

Flanagan, R.J., Soskice, D.W. and Ulman, L. (1983), *Unionism, Economic Stabilization and Income Policies: European Experience*, Brookings Institution, Washington.

Franz, W. (1990a), 'Hysteresis and Economic Relationship: An Overview' in Franz (ed.) (1990b).

Franz W. (ed.) (1990b), *Hysteresis Effects in Economic Models*, Physica-Verlag, Heidelberg, New York.

Frey, B.S. and Schneider, F. (1978), 'A Politico-Economic Model of the United Kingdom', *Economic Journal*, vol. 88, June, pp. 243–53.

Friedman, M. (1966), 'What Price Guidepost?', in Schulz and Aliber (eds), (1966).

Friedman, M. (1968), 'The Role of Monetary Policy', *American Economic Review*, vol. 58, no. 1, March, pp. 1–17.

Friedman, M. (1975), 'Unemployment vs. Inflation? An Evaluation of the Phillips Curve', *IEA Occasional Paper no. 44*, reprinted in Friedman (1991), pp. 63–86.

Friedman, M. (1977), 'Inflation and Unemployment', *IEA Occasional Paper no. 51*, reprinted in Friedman (1991), pp. 87–111.

Friedman, M. (1991), *Monetarist Economics*, Blackwell, Oxford.

Frisch, H. (1983), *Theories of Inflation*, Cambridge University Press.

Frydman, R. and Phelps, E.S. (1983a), *Introduction*, in Frydman and Phelps (eds) (1983b), pp. 1–30.

Frydman, R. and Phelps, E.S. (eds) (1983b), *Individual Forecasting and Aggregate Outcomes*, Cambridge University Press, New York.

Galbraith, J.K. (1997) 'Time to Ditch the NAIRU', *Journal of Economic Perspectives*, vol. 11, no. 1, Winter, pp. 93–108.

Giersch, H. (1987), 'Economic Policies in the Age of Schumpeter', *European Economic Review*, vol. 31, pp. 35–52.

Gordon, R.J. (ed.) (1972), *Milton Friedman's Monetary Framework. A Debate with His Critics*, University of Chicago Press, Chicago.

Gordon, R.J. (1981), *Macroeconomics*, Little Brown and Company, Boston, Toronto.

Gordon, R.J. (1989), 'Hysteresis in History: Was There Ever a Phillips Curve?', *American Economic Review*, vol. 79, no. 2, May, pp. 220-5.

Gordon, R.J. (1997), 'The Time-Varying NAIRU and its Implications for Economic Policy', *Journal of Economic Perspectives*, vol. 11, no. 1, Winter, pp. 11–32.

Grossman, H.I. (1972), 'Was Keynes a "Keynesian"? A Review Article', *Journal of Economic Literature*, vol. 10, no. 1, March, pp. 25–30.

Grossman, H.I. (1974), 'The Cyclical Pattern of Unemployment and Wage Inflation', *Economica*, no. 41, November, pp. 403–13.

Grubb, D. (1986), 'Topics in the OECD Phillips Curve', *Economic Journal*, vol. 96, no. 381, March, pp. 55–79.

Grubb, D., Jackman, R. and Layard, R. (1982), 'Causes of the Current Stagflation', *Review of Economic Studies*, October, pp. 707–730.

Gylfason, T. and Lindbeck, A. (1982), The Political Economy of Cost-Inflation, *Kyklos*, vol. 35, no. 3, pp. 430–55.

Hahn, F.H. (1993), 'Il futuro del capitalismo: segni premonitori', *Rivista milanese di economia*, aprile–giugno.

148 *Inflation, unemployment and money*

Hahn, F.H. and Brechling, F. (eds), (1965), *International Economic Association Series*, Macmillan, London.

Hahn, F.H. and Solow, R. (1995), *A Critical Essay on Modern Macroeconomic Theory*, MIT Press, Cambridge, Mass.

Hall, R.E. (1975), 'The Rigidity of Wages and the Persistence of Unemployment', *Brookings Papers on Economic Activity*, no. 2.

Hall, R.E. (1980), 'Employment, Fluctuations and Wage Rigidities', *Brooking Papers on Economic Activity*, no. 1, pp. 91–124.

Hall, R.E. and Taylor J.B. (1988), *Macroeconomics*, Norton & Co., New York.

Haltiwanger, J.C. (1983), 'On the Relationship between Risk Aversion and the Development of Long-Term Worker-Firm Attachment', *Southern Economic Journal*, October, pp. 572–7.

Haltiwanger, J.C. (1987), 'Natural Rate of Unemployment', in Eatwell, Milgate, Newman, (1987), pp. 610–12.

Hansen, B. (1970), 'Excess Demand, Unemployment, Vacancies and Wages', *Quarterly Journal of Economics*, vol. 84, no. 1, February, pp. 1–23.

Hargreaves Heap, S.P. (1980), 'Choosing the Wrong "Natural Rate": Accelerating Inflation or Decelerating Employment and Growth', *Economic Journal*, vol. 90, no. 359, September, pp. 611–620.

Healey, N.M. (1988), 'L'esperimento monetarista del 1979-1982 nel regno Unito: perché gli economisti continuano a non essere d'accordo', *Moneta e credito*, vol. 41, no. 161, pp. 887–117.

Henley, A. and Tsakalotos (1993), *Corporatism and Economic Performance*, Edward Elgar, Aldershot.

Henley, A. and Tsakalotos (1995), 'Unemployment Experience and the Institutional Preconditions for Full Employment', in Arestis and Marshall (eds) (1995), pp. 176–201.

Hicks, J.R. (1963), *The Theory of Wages*, 2nd ed., Macmillan, London.

Hicks, J. (1974), *The Crisis in Keynesian Economics*, Basil Blackwell, Oxford.

Hines, A.G. (1964), 'Trade Unions and Wage Inflation in the United Kingdom, 1893-1961', *Review of Economic Studies*, vol. 31, October, pp. 221–52.

Hines, A.G.(1971), 'The Determinants of the Rate of Change of Money Wage Rates and the Effectiveness of Income Policy', in Johnson and Nobay (eds) (1971), pp. 143–75.

Holmes, J.M. and Smyth, D.J. (1970), 'The Relation Between Unemployment and Excess Demand for Labour: an Examination of the Theory of the Phillips Curve', *Economica*, vol. 37, no. 147, August, pp. 311–15.

Holt, C.C. (1970), 'Job Search, Phillips Wage Relation, and Union Influence', in Phelps (ed.) (1970b), pp. 53–123.

Hotelling, H. (1929), 'Stability in Competition', *Economic Journal*, vol. 39, no. 153, March, pp. 41–57.

Hutchison, T.W. (1977), *Keynes versus 'Keynesians'?*, IEA, London.

Isaac, A.G. (1993), 'Is There a Natural Rate?', *Journal of Post Keynesian Economics*, vol. 15, no. 4, Summer, pp. 453–70.

Jackman, R.A., Layard, P.R.G. and Pissarides, C. (1986), 'Policies for Reducing the Natural Rate of Unemployment', in Butkiewicz, Koford and Miller (eds), (1986), pp. 111–52.

Jackman, R.A., Mulvey, C. and Trevitick, A.J. (1981), *The Economics of Inflation*, Basil Blackwell, Oxford.

Jenkinson, T. (1987), 'The Natural Rate of Unemployment: Does it Exist?', *Oxford Review of Economic Policy*, vol. 3, no. 3, pp. 20–6.

Jenkinson, T. (1990), 'The Assessment: Inflation Policy', *Oxford Review of Economic Policy*, vol. 6, no. 4, pp. 1–14.

Johnson, H.G. (1972), *Inflation and the Monetarist Controversy*, North-Holland, Amsterdam.

Johnson, G.E. and Layard, R. (1986), 'The Natural Rate of Unemployment: Explanation and Policy', in Ashenfelter (1986), pp. 921–99.

Johnson, H.G. and Nobay, A.R. (eds) (1971), *The Current Inflation*, Macmillan, London.

Jones, A. (1973), *The New Inflation: the Politics of Prices and Incomes*, Penguin Books, Harmondsworth.

Jones, S.R.G. (1995), *The Persistence of Unemployment. Hysteresis in Canadian Labour Markets*, McGill-Queen's University Press, Montreal.

Jossa, B. (1989), 'Class Struggle and Income Distribution in Kaleckian Theory', in Sebastiani (ed.) (1989), pp. 142–54.

Jossa, B. (1992), 'Keynesian Unemployment is Involuntary and is an Equilibrium State', in Sebastiani (ed.) (1992), pp. 120–37.

Jossa, B. and Musella, M. (1992), 'La curva di Phillips: una sintesi di trent'anni di discussioni', in Jossa and Nardi (eds) (1992), pp. 103–52.

Jossa, B. and Musella, M. (1995), 'Curva di Phillips, isteresi e teoria keynesiana', in Amendola (ed.) (1995), pp. 125–50.

Jossa, B. and Nardi, A. (eds) (1992), *Lezioni di macroeconomia*, Il Mulino, Bologna.

Juhn, C., Murphy, K.M. and Topel, R.H. (1991), 'Why Has the Natural Rate of Unemployment Increased over Time?', in *Brookings Papers on Economic Activity*, no. 2, pp. 75–126.

Kaldor, N. and Trevithick, J. (1981), 'A Keynesian Perspective on Money', *Lloyds Bank Review*, vol. 139, January, pp. 1–19.

Kalecki, M. (1939), 'Money and Real Wages', in Kalecki (1991), pp. 21–50.

Kalecki, M. (1943), 'Political Aspects of Full Employment', in Kalecki (1990), pp. 345–56.

Kalecki, M. (1971), 'Class Struggle and Distribution of Income', in Kalecki (1991), pp. 96–103.

Kalecki, M. (1990), *Collected Works,* vol. I, 'Capitalism. Cycles and Full Employment', Oxford University Press, Oxford

Kalecki, M. (1991), *Collected Works,* vol. II, 'Capitalism. Economic Dynamics', Oxford University Press, Oxford

Kaliski, S.F. (1964), 'The Relation Between Unemployment and the Rate of Change of Money Wages in Canada, *International Economic Review,* vol. 5, vol. 1, January, pp. 1–33.

Katzener, D.W. (1993), 'Some Notes of the Role of History and the Definition of Hysteresis and Related Concepts, *Journal of Post Keynesian Economics,* vol. 15, no. 3, Spring, pp. 323–46.

Keynes, J.M. (1936), *The General Theory of Employment, Interest and Money,* Macmillan, London, edition 1973.

Keynes, J.M. (1940), 'How to Pay for the War', in Keynes (1973), pp. 367–439.

Keynes, J.M. (1973), *The Collected Writings of J.M. Keynes ,* vol. IX, Macmillan, London.

Kirschgassner, G. (1984), 'On the Theory of Optimal Government Behaviour', *Journal of Economic Dynamics and Control,* no. 4, pp. 167–95.

Klein, L.R. and Ball, R.J. (1959), 'Some Econometrics of the Determination of Absolute Prices Wages', *Economic Journal,* vol. 69, no. 275, September, pp. 467–82.

Koford, K.J. and Miller, J.B. (1992), 'Macroeconomic Market Incentive Plans: History and Theoretical Rationale', *American Economic Review,* vol. 82, no. 2, May, pp. 330–4.

Kramer, G.M. (1977), 'A Dynamic Model of Political Equilibrium', *Journal of Economic Theory,* vol. 16, no. 2, December, pp. 310–34.

Krashewski, R.S. (1988), 'What is so Natural about High Unemployment', in *American Economic Review,* vol. 78, no. 2, May, pp. 289–93.

Kydland, F.E and Prescott, E.C. (1977), 'Rules Rather than Discretion: The Inconsistency of Optimal Plan', *Journal of Political Economy,* vol. 85, no. 3, June, pp. 473–91.

Laidler, D. (1971), 'The Phillips Curve, Expectations and Incomes Policy', in Johnson and Nobay (eds), (1971), pp. 75–98.

Lavoie, M. (1993), *Foundations of Post Keynesian Economic Analysis,* Edward Elgar, Aldershot.

Lawrence, R.Z., Schultze, C.L. (1988), *Barriers to European Growth: a Transatlantic View,* Brookings Institution, Washington.

Layard, R. and Calmfors, L. (eds) (1987), *The Fight Against Unemployment*, MIT Press, Cambridge, Mass.

Layard, R. and Nickell, S. (1985), 'The Causes of British Unemployment', *National Istitute Economic Review*, no. 111, February, pp. 62–85.

Layard, R. and Nickell, S. (1986), 'Unemployment in Britain', in Bean, Layard and Nickell (eds) (1986), pp. 121–69.

Layard, R. and Nickell, S. (1987), 'The Labour Market', in Dornbusch and Layard (eds) (1987), pp. 131–79.

Layard, R., Nickell, S. and Jackman, R. (1991), *Unemployment. Macroeconomic Performance and Labour Market*, Oxford University Press, Oxford.

Leeson, R. (1994), 'The Rise and Fall of Keynesian Economics', *Economic Record*, vol. 70, no. 210, September, pp. 249–53.

Leeson, R. (1997), 'Does the Expectations Trap Render the Natural-Rate Model Invalid in the Disinflationary Zone?', *Cambridge Journal of Economics*, 21, 1, pp. 95–101.

Lerner, A.P., Colander, D.C. (1979), 'Map: a Cure for Inflation', in Colander (ed.) (1979), pp. 493-503.

Lipsey, R.G. (1960), 'The Relation between Unemployment and the Rate of Change of Money Wage Rates in the United Kingdom, 1862–1957: a Further Analysis', *Economica*, vol. 27, no. 105, February, pp. 1–31.

Lipsey, R.G. (1974), 'The Micro Theory of the Phillips Curve Reconsidered: a Reply to Holmes and Smyth', *Economica*, vol. 41, no. 161, February, pp. 62–70.

Lipsey, R.G. (1978), *The Place of Phillips Curve in Macro-Models*, in Bergstrom *et al.* (1978), pp. 49–75.

Lord Beveridge (1944), *Full Employment in a Free Society. A Report by Lord Beveridge*, George Allen & Unwin, London.

Lucas, R.E. (1973), 'Some International Evidence on Output-Inflation Trade-offs', *American Economic Review*, vol. 63, no. 3, June, pp. 326–34.

Maddock, R. and Carter, M. (1981–82), 'Inflation as a Prisoner's Dilemma: a Comment', *Journal of Post Keynesian Economics*, vol. 4, no. 2, Winter, pp. 330–1.

Maddock, R. and Carter, M. (1982), 'A Child's Guide to Rational Expectations', *Journal of Economic Literature*, vol. 20, no. 1, March, pp. 39–51.

Maital, S. and Benjaminini, Y. (1980), 'Inflation as Prisoner's Dilemma', *Journal of Post Keynesian Economics*, vol. 2, no. 4, Summer, pp. 459–81.

Malinvaud, E. (1984), *Mass Unemployment*, Basil Blackwell, Oxford.

Mankiw, N.G. (1993), 'Symposium on Keynesian Economics Today', in *Journal of Economic Perspectives*, vol. 7, no. 1, Winter, pp. 3–4.

Marglin, J.B. (1984), 'Growth, Distribution and Inflation: a Centennial Syntesis', *Cambridge Journal of Economics*, vol. 8, no. 2, June, pp. 115–44.

Marx, K. (1867), *Capital: A Critique of Political Economy*, vol. I, Penguin Books, London, 1976.

McCallum, B.T. (1977), 'The Political Business Cycle: an Empirical Test', *Southern Economic Journal*, vol. 43, January, pp. 504–15.

McCallum, B.T. (1996), *International Monetary Economics*, Oxford University Press, New York.

McCallum, J. (1983), 'Inflation and Social Consensus in the Seventies', *Economic Journal*, vol. 93, December, pp. 784–805.

McCallum, J. (1986), 'Unemployment in OECD Countries in the 1980s', *Economic Journal*, vol. 96, December, pp. 942–60.

Mc Connel, C.R. and Brue, S.R. (1995), *Contemporary Labor Economics*, McGraw-Hill, London.

Mc Donald, I. (1995), 'Models of the Range of Equilibria', in Cross (ed.) (1995), pp. 101–52.

Meade, J.E. (1982), *Stagflation*, vol. 1, 'Wage-Fixing', George Allen & Unwin, London.

Miller, J. (ed.) (1994), *The Rational Expectations Revolution*, MIT Press, Cambridge, Mass.

Minford, P. and Peel, D. (1981), 'The Role of Monetary Stabilization Policy under Rational Expectations', *The Manchester School of Economics*, vol. 49, no. 1, March, pp. 39-49.

Minford, P. and Peel, D. (1983), *Rational Expectations and the Macroeconomics*, Martin Robertson, Oxford.

Minford, P. and Riley, J. (1994), *The U.K. Labour Market: Micro - Rigidities and Macro Obstructions*, in Barrel (ed.) (1994), pp. 258–72.

Modigliani, F. (1977), 'The Monetarist Controversy, or Should We Forsake Stabilization Policies?', in *American Economic Review*, vol. 67, no. 2, pp. 1–19.

Modigliani, F. and Papademus, L. (1975), 'Targets for Monetary Policy in the Coming Year', in *Brookings Papers on Economic Activity*, vol. 6, no. 1, pp. 141–63.

Mortensen, D.T. (1986), 'Job Search and Labour Market Analysis', in Ashenfelter (ed.) (1986), Vol II.

Musella, M. (1988a), 'Inflazione e conflitto sociale in un modello *alla Rowthorn*', *Rivista di politica economica*, vol. 78, no. 12, dicembre, pp. 1352–72.

Musella, M. (1988b), 'La curva di Phillips derivata da un modello kaleckiano', *Studi economici*, vol. 43, no. 35, pp. 105–128.

Musella, M. (1992a), 'A proposito di un recente libro di macroeconomia', *Giornale degli economisti e Annali di economia*, vol. 51 (n.s.), no. 5–8, maggio-agosto, pp. 281–94.

Musella, M. (1992b), 'Offerta di moneta, politica monetaria e inflazione da conflitto', in Arcelli (ed.) (1992), pp. 139–56.

Myatt, A. (1986), 'On the Non-Existence of a Natural Rate of Unemployment and Kaleckian Micro Underpinnings to the Phillips Curve', *Journal of Post Keynesian Economics*, vol. 18, no. 3, Spring, pp. 447–62.

Napoleoni, C. (1966), 'Politica dei redditi e programmazione', *La Rivista Trimestrale*, no. 17-18; reprinted in Napoleoni (1992), pp. 77–98.

Napoleoni, C. (1992), *Dalla scienza all'utopia*, Boringhieri, Torino.

Nell, E. (1985), 'Jean Baptiste Marglin: a Comment on *Growth, Distribution and Inflation*', *Cambridge Journal of Economics*, vol. 9, no. 2, June, pp. 173–8.

Nevile, J.W. (1979), 'How Voluntary is Unemployment? Two Views of the Phillips Curve', *Journal of Post Keynesian Economics*, vol. 2, no. 1, Autumn, pp. 110–9.

Nordhaus, W.D. (1975), 'The Political Business Cycle', *Review of Economic Studies*, vol. 42, April, pp. 169–90.

Oswald, J. (1985), 'The Economic Theory of Trade Unions. An Introduction', *Scandinavian Journal of Economics*, vol. 87, no. 2, pp. 160–93.

Paish, F.W. (1971), *Rise and Fall of Incomes Policy*, IEA, Hobert Paper 47, London.

Palley, T. (1996), *Postkeynesian Economics*, Macmillan, London.

Patinkin, D. (1965), *Money, Interest and Prices (An Integration of Monetary and Value Theory)*, A Harper International Edition, Illinois.

Pekkarin, J., Pohjula, M. and Rowthorn, B. (eds) (1992), 'Introduction', in *Social Corporatism: A Superior Economic System*, Clarendon Press, Oxford.

Phelps, E.S. (1967), 'Phillips Curves, Expectations of Inflation, and Optimal Unemployment Over Time', *Economica*, vol. 34, no. 135, August, pp. 254–81.

Phelps, E.S. (1969), 'The New Microeconomics in Inflation and Employment Theory', *American Economic Review*, vol. 59, no. 2, May, pp. 147–60.

Phelps, E.S. (1970a), 'Introduction: the New Microeconomics in Employment and Inflation Theory', in Phelps (ed.) (1970b), pp. 1–23.

Phelps, E.S. (ed.) (1970b), *Microeconomic Foundations of Employment and Inflation Theory*, Norton & Co., New York.

Phelps, E.S. (1970c), *Money Wage Dynamics and Labour Market Equilibrium*, in Phelps (ed.) (1970b), pp. 124–66.

Phelps, E.S. (1972), *Inflation Policy and Unemployment Theory*, London.

Phelps, E.S. (1994), *Structural Slumps*, Cambridge, Harward University Press.

Phelps, E.S. (1995), 'The Origins and Further Development of the Natural Rate of Unemployment', in Cross (ed.) (1995b), pp. 15–31.

Phillips, A.W. (1958), 'The Relation Between Unemployment and the Rate of Change of Money Wage Rates in the United Kingdom, 1861–1957', *Economica*, vol. 25, no. 100, November, pp. 283–99.

Pissarides, C. (1986), *Comment by Christopher Pissarides*, in Butkiewicz, Koford and Miller (eds) (1986), pp. 55–7.

Pissarides, C.A. (1990), *Equilibrium Unemployment Theory*, Basil Blackwell, Oxford.

Pohjula , M. (1992), 'Corporatism and Wage Bargaining', in Pekkarin, Pohjula and Rowthorn, (eds), (1992).

Rasmusen, E. (1990), *Games and Information*, Basil Blackwell, Oxford.

Rees, A. (1970), 'The Phillips Curve as a Menu for Political Choice', *Economica*, vol. 37, no. 147, August, pp. 227–38.

Riach, P.A. (1995), 'Wage-employment Determination in a Post-Keynesian World', in Arestis and Marshall (eds) (1995), pp. 163–75.

Roncaglia, A. (1986), *Le politiche dei redditi: introduzione a un dibattito*, Banca Popolare dell'Etruria, Arezzo.

Routh, G. (1959) 'The Relation Between Unemployment and The Rate of Change of Money Wage Rates: A Comment', *Economica*, no. 26, November, pp. 299–315.

Rowthorn, R.E. (1977), *Conflict, Inflation and Money*, in Rowthorn, 1980, pp. 148–81.

Rowthorn, R.E. (1980), *Capitalism, Conflict and Inflation*, Lawrence & Wishart, London.

Rowthorn, R.E. (1995), *Capital Formation and Unemployment*, ESRC Centre for Business Research, WP 7, May.

Rowthorn, R.E. (1996), *Unemployment, Wage Bargaining and Capital-Labour Substitution*, Paper presented at AIEL Annual Conference.

Salop, S.C. (1973), 'Systematic Job Search and Unemployment', *Review of Economic Studies*, vol. 40, no. 2, April, pp. 191–201.

Salop, S. C. (1979), 'A Model of The Natural Rate of Unemployment', *American Economic Review*, vol. 69, no. 1, March, pp. 117–25.

Salvati, M. (1981), 'Ciclo politico e onde lunghe. Note su Kalecki e Phelps Brown', *Stato e Mercato*, vol. 1, no. 1, pp. 9–46.

Samuelson, P.A. and Solow R.M. (1960), 'Analytical Aspects of Anti-Inflation Policy', *American Economic Review*, vol. 50, no. 2, May, pp. 177–94.

Santomero, A.M. and Seater, J.J. (1978), 'The Inflation-Unemployment Trade Off: a Critique of the Literature', *Journal of Economic Literature*, vol. 16, no. 2, June, pp. 499–544.

Sargent, T.J. (1976), 'A Classical Macroeconomic Model for the United States', *Journal of Political Economy*, vol. 84, no. 2, April, pp.207–37.

Sargent, T.J. and Wallace, N. (1975), 'Rational Expectations, the Optimal Monetary Instruments and the Optimal Money Supply Rule', *Journal of Political Economy*, vol. 83, no. 2, April, pp. 241–544.

Sargent, T.J., and Wallace, N. (1976), 'Rational Expectations and the Theory of Economic Policy', *Journal of Monetary Economics*, vol. 2, no. 2, April, pp. 169–83.

Sawyer, M. (1985), *The Economics of Michael Kalecki*, Macmillan, London.

Sawyer, M. (1995), 'Obstacles to Full Employment in Capitalist Economies', in Arestis and Marshall (1995), pp. 15–35.

Scandizzo, P.L. (ed.) (1992), *La politica dei redditi in Italia*, ISPE, Roma.

Schulz G.P. and Aliber R.Z. (eds) (1966), *Guidelines: Informal Controls and the Market Place*, University of Chicago Press, Chicago.

Scitovsky, T. (1978), 'Market Power and Inflation', *Economica*, vol. 45, no. 179, August, pp. 221–33.

Screpanti, E. (1996), 'A Pure Insider Theory of Hysteresis in Employment and Unemployment', *Review of Radical Political Economics*, vol. 28, no. 4, pp. 93–112.

Sebastiani, M. (1985), *L'equilibrio di sottoccupazione nel pensiero di Michael Kalecki*, La Nuova Italia Scientifica, Roma.

Sebastiani, M. (ed.) (1989), *Kalecki's Relevance Today*, Macmillan, London.

Sebastiani, M. (ed.) (1992), *The Notion of Equilibrium in Keynesian Theory*, Macmillan, London.

Setterfield, M. (1993), 'Toward a Long Run Theory of Effective Demand: Modelling Macroeconomics System with Hysteresis', *Journal of Post Keynesian Economics*, vol. 15, no. 3, Spring, pp. 347–86.

Sheffrin, S.M. (1983), *Rational Expectations*, Cora Ed., Cambridge.

Sinclair, P. (1987), *Unemployment; Economic Theory and Evidence*, Basil Blackwell, Oxford.

Skott, P. (1989), *Conflict and Effective Demand in Economic Growth*, Cambridge University Press, Cambridge, Mass.

Smith, S.W. (1994), *Labour Economics*, Routledge, Amsterdam.

Solow, R.M. (1977), *Inflazione: guida per il cittadino intelligente*, Società Editrice Subalpina, Torino.

Staiger, D., Stock, J.H. and Watson, M.W. (1997), 'The NAIRU, Unemployment and Monetary Policy', *Journal of Economic Perspectives*, vol. 11, no. 1, Winter, pp. 33–50.

Stevenson, A., Muscatelli, V. and Gregory, M. (1988), *Macroeconomic Theory and Stabilization Policy*, Philip Allan Publishers Ltd, Oxford.

Stiglitz, J. (1997) 'Reflection on the Natural Rate Hypothesis', *Journal of Economic Perspectives*, vol. 11, no. 1, Winter, pp. 3–10.

Summers, L.H. (1986), 'Why is the Unemployment Rate so Very High Near Full Employment?', *Brookings Papers on Economic Activity*, no. 2, pp. 339–83.

Summers, L.H. (1988), 'Should Keynesian Economics Dispense with the Phillips Curve?', in Cross (ed.) (1988), pp. 11–25.

Sutcliffe, C. (1982), 'Inflation as Prisoner's Dilemma', *Journal of Post Keynesian Economics*, vol. 5, no. 4, Summer, pp. 574–85.

Sylos Labini, P. (1974), *Trade Unions, Inflation and Productivity*, Lexington Books, Lexington, Mass.

Sylos Labini, P. (1984), *The Forces of Economic Growth and Decline*, MIT Press, Cambridge, Mass.

Sylos Labini, P. (1985), 'Weintraub on the Price Level and Macroeconomics', *Journal of Post Keynesian Economics*, vol. 7, no. 4, Summer, pp. 559–74.

Tarantelli, E. (1974), *Studi di economia del lavoro*, Giuffrè, Milano.

Tarantelli, E. (1981), 'Politiche di rientro e inflazione nei paesi industrializzati e il ruolo economico del sindacato', *Laboratorio Politico*, no. 4, pp. 174–99.

Tarantelli, E. (1986), *Economia politica del lavoro*, Utet, Torino.

Tarling, R.J. and Wilkinson, F. (1977), 'The Social Contract: Postwar Income Policies and their Inflationary Impact', *Cambridge Journal of Economics*, vol. 1, no. 4, December, pp. 395–414.

Telser, L.G. (1973), 'Searching for the Lowest Price', *American Economic Review*, vol. 163, no. 2, May, pp. 40–51.

Tobin, J. (1972), 'Friedman's Theoretical Framework', in Gordon (ed.) (1972).

Tobin, J. (1977), 'How Dead is Keynes?', *Economic Inquiry*, October, pp. 459–68.

Tobin, J. (1980a), *Asset Accumulation and Economic Activity*, Basil Blackwell, Oxford.

Tobin, J. (1980b), 'Real Balance Effect Reconsidered', in Tobin (1980a).

Tobin, J. (1980c), 'Stabilization Policy Ten Years After', *Brookings Papers on Economic Activity*, no. 1.

Tobin, J. (1995), 'The Natural Rate as New Classical Macroeconomics', in Cross (ed.) (1995b), pp. 32–42.

Turchscherer, T. (1979), 'Keynes' Model and the Keynesians: A Synthesis', *Journal of Post Keynesian Economics*, vol. 1, no. 4, pp. 96–109.

Turchscherer, T. (1984), 'Meltzer on Keynes's Labor Market Theory: A Review of the *General Theory's* Second Chapter', *Journal of Post Keynesian Economics*, vol. 4, no. 4, pp. 523–31.

Vanderkamp, J. (1968), 'The Phillips Relation: a Theoretical Explanation: a Comment', *Economica*, vol. 35, no. 138, May, pp. 179–83.

Vickrey, W. (1961), 'The Burden of Public Debt: Comment', *American Economic Review*, vol. 51, no. 1, March, pp. 132–7.

Vickrey, W. (1992), 'Chock-Full Employment without Increased Inflation: a Proposal for Marketable Markup Warrants', *American Economic Review*, vol. 82, no. 2, May, pp. 341–59.

Weintraub, S. (1958), *An Approach to the Theory of Income Distribution*, Chilton Company, Philadelphia.

Weintraub, S. (1960), 'The Keynesian Theory of Inflation: the Two Faces of Janus?', *International Economic Review*, vol. 1, no. 2, May, pp. 143–55.

Weintraub, S. (1978a), *Capitalism's Inflation and Unemployment Crisis*, Addison Wesley, Reading, Mass.

Weintraub, S. (1978b), *Keynes, Keynesians and Monetarists*, University of Pennsylvania Press, Philadelphia.

Wulwick, N.J. (1996), 'Two Econometrics Replications: The Historic Phillips and Lipsey-Phillips Curves', *History of Political Economy*, vol. 28, no. 3, pp. 391–437.

Wyplosz, C. (1987), 'Comments' in Layard and Calmfors (eds) (1987).

Index

159